Leadership,
The Path to Success

By

William B. Gilmore, MRCP, MPA

DEDICATION

To leaders who have walked in my footsteps,

Who acknowledge the dedication of purpose,

Understand that you must drive to achieve change,

And no true leader will come out unscathed.

ACKNOWLEDGMENT

This is a book crafted from experience where the tools of battle are your sense of purpose, ability to communicate, ethical balance facing political headwinds, being part of a team that wants positive change where mediocracy is the standard, and a desire to be valued individually, representing your team who trust in your vision and share it with enthusiasm. My experience has benefited from a variety of men and women who have seen my value, have mentored my development, and have applauded my success. Your work life is not an individual sport but a shared passion involving talented individuals who fill the gaps in your own capabilities that build metrics justifying that you have attained successful outcomes.

Table of Contents

Prologue

The attention of this book is to focus on leadership issues in the public sector. Essentially, the area of local, municipal, school, state, and legislative government is seriously in need of long-term strategic leadership engagement, embracing:

- Being humble yet confident in your opinion,

- Creativity built on team thinking,

- Measured risk-taking while being brutally honest and demonstrating fierce resolve,

- Efficiencies using technology to streamline services and improve labor utilization,

- Expounding on the value of communication, which emphasizes listening and the tone of your delivery when speaking,

- The importance of data tracking needed to trend outcomes that drive the next steps used to pursue a team's original intent and shared vision and

- An understanding of solid fiscal management which is central to any sustainable organization.

In today's economy, public life, and representative government, leadership is not adequately represented. Leaders need to have the willingness to take risks that challenge public boards, elected officials, strong-willed department heads, and an uninformed public. They cannot be in a position where they are waiting to be told what needs to be done. Their energy must drive activities that push the management team toward the attainment of a shared vision. Practicing an independent nature must work in tandem with boards and committees that expect management to follow their lead. Yet, practicing a degree of independence allows the leader the opportunity to influence change that aligns with their professional position, goalposts, guardrails, and the fiscal reality shared by their management team. It is something that is not being taught effectively enough to any real degree in many universities and in advanced degrees in Public Administration.

The promotion of a social contract between leadership and the body politic is valuable for building trust in government. A contract promoted by leadership creates, builds, and supports a shared vision based on a team approach. The benefit of an agreement that pulls ideas, volunteerism, and shared priorities, along with long-term strategic plans matching a vision of funding realities, will go a long way toward creating a brave new world — essentially, a path to success.

Why the choice to describe my perspective on leadership, the need for it, the challenge it is for many, and why the lack of it represents a vulnerability in our broad community of public entities? In my experience — limited in some ways and broad in others — the public sector fails to attract enough thoughtful, talented, caring, and sensitive individuals who are open to communication, operate as team players, and demonstrate a value-driven professional attitude, putting the public before themselves. This type of leader avoids being labeled as self-centered, narcissistic, weak-backed, or a bootlicking personality who lacks a sincere moral compass and demonstrates a willingness to follow poor directives against their own professional perspective.

Most importantly, there is an immediate need for an empathetic personality who establishes their position with the ruling body as a decision-maker — one who understands their responsibility to the community to control budget expenditures, is willing to accept and respond to input from their department heads, will challenge these same individuals to meet assigned benchmarks that measure progress, and will establish a pay scale that attracts professional talent who share this management philosophy. However, there are leaders who share a desire to achieve progress but demonstrate a lack of confidence and the basic instinct to push risk-taking. They tend to succumb to pushback from councils and boards, avoiding pressing for real change in the face of pressure to avoid rate or tax increases, even though new spending and policy changes may ultimately provide real value to the community and the organization generally.

The judgment to air this story is based on my own work experience, where I drove each organization to change — or else. I led in a direction I knew was needed to create a new standard of management and ensured that I left the organization in better shape than when I arrived. The anecdotes outlined in the following pages provide an overview of the journey I followed. The situations will concern anyone serious about creating a valued social contract embracing the love of a neighbor, the value of self-respect, the usefulness of being valued and heard, and an understanding of being part of a large community of morally guided members of society. The journey is also one of hope and acceptance — specifically, earning respect for one another to overcome the challenges life presents, which is a never-ending process of personal growth.

But as we all know, it takes a community to build guardrails that allow everyone to align themselves on the side of cooperation, coordination, opportunity, and the concept of shared values that put us all on the same page, wanting the same outcome. Understanding that every person in the community has capabilities that make each of us unique is key. Defining the role of leaders who have the natural capacity to draw on those unique talents and perceive the road ahead allows the rest, who are building the value of community existence, to follow and support the trusted personalities in leadership roles.

What I have learned is that there are fewer trusted individuals in leadership roles than there should be. Many are deliberately installed because certain groups want a minority to control the majority through subtle selection backed by a small number of similarly weak guidelines. Instinct dictates fighting that type of control. Being better at communicating a message of hope—both written and vocal—and using progressive points of success to demonstrate the value of open leadership is crucial. The selection of lieutenants who are willing to avoid attempts at control by minority members seeking power for themselves is equally important.

Schools at all levels do not build or teach enough capacity for leaders to grow into morally driven personalities. That is the message I hope to offer through my story of work experience. I want others to understand why it is important to push back on weak programming and policy matters. Pursuing an avenue that drives change—rather than waiting to be told what should be done—prevents the weakening of the progressive nature of a true change agent.

This is the purpose of describing my story. It required a degree of sleuthing closely aligned with performing a forensic audit. The audit process uses work conditions to provide the baseline for building a progressive document of findings, used to overcome—not necessarily in all cases—the successive walls of the board or council obstruction. These obstructions attempt to control and limit progress when the true purpose of progress is to grow effectively and efficiently within a reasonable spending program.

The Making of a Leadership Sleuth

Introduction

Leadership opportunities can be experienced in many ways: by appointment, by election, by choice when acknowledged in a committee or group setting, by demonstration of confidence when faced with a difficult decision that others find challenging, and so on. Whatever way you are placed in that role, it can range from both exciting to terrifying, yet the outcome is the same — you are still in charge or in a position of influence, and making the best of the situation is a choice to be made, not necessarily the easiest road taken. Of critical importance is understanding who you are, your personal value that grounds you and substantiates your confidence to be in a leadership position, understanding the degree of moral and ethical persuasion that you will accept and live by, and determining your vision of what you want to provide and drive toward in a role that you may accept without reservation. Deep down, you have already planned or designed your vision of what you want to achieve — next month, next year, or longer. It is not written in stone, but you know, deep down, that you will be putting the program, organization, key associates, and others on a trail that benefits everyone despite the efforts of other deniers of positive change.

The beginning of my journey toward an understanding of leadership follows what I have determined to be my natural life pursuit. This is grounded in my belief that leadership is earned and not planned nor required to fill a lead role. It is my belief and my learned perspective that "leaders aren't born, they are made." (Vince Lombardi). Experiences over the course of my life have been surprising and eventful at unexpected times when I have been put into a lead role to comment, decide, determine, analyze, coordinate, build consensus, and commit myself and/or the organization to a strategic direction. I learned from family meals, church, sports, acting in theatre, high school debate team, Boy Scouts, traveling to foreign countries during my youth, and understanding the importance of reading more than one source document to get a broader understanding of the issues driving a movement. My father, who had worked for the U.S. State Department and was a professor of history who remained engaged as a consultant to the former agency during his teaching career, was very good at pushing our relatively naïve stances on topics, questioning us suggestively into a new understanding that saw me doing more work to correct my fallacies and gaps in learning.

There are key times in everyone's life when the opportunity for leadership is thrust upon them. When it happens, are they someone who steps up to handle the role they've been given, or are they a reluctant placeholder looking for a way to transfer responsibility to someone else? Just as I am a person who sees life from the perspective of a glass half full, the chance of leadership was something I felt confident performing, even though there were many times I was overlooked due to my outgoing nature, where I sensed that I couldn't be taken seriously. The key to taking on a leadership role, from my experience, is to have the confidence to face a problem and approach it directly, query your peers to generate alternatives, know how much you can commit to (i.e., time, budget, equipment, staff), and own the outcome if it goes wrong but share success with all involved. I also learned that it isn't necessarily critical to be the lead person in any team or committee exchange. There are times when you need to be the first to comment on a central topic to establish an initial position that can be built upon and improved so that all share in the success of the outcome. A second approach is to wait to hear what others offer so that you can step in to consolidate the earlier discussion into a viable proposal that pulls comments from everyone and, again, provides the opportunity to share success with the group. This is subtle leadership, and it is something others recognize and will rely on during other events.

One of my mentors told me that there are only two things that come out of any meeting, no matter the size or purpose. Basically, you either earn more or less respect. Respect can only be earned and not demanded by anyone. Many leaders miss that nuance. Earned respect also allows a level of trust to accumulate as you demonstrate over time, with repeated levelheaded and common-sense actions, that we can all do better if we follow our leader.

The success of any leader also comes down to communication and how well you do it. Anyone can speak and tell their story. However, getting your target audience to listen and get behind your mission requires an approach that builds respect and trust, as discussed above. The tone of your message — your voice and the demeanor of your stance in front of your audience — tells a lot about you and the confidence you have in your subject matter. Your voice needs to be both strong and relaxed. Your eyes need to be on the audience, not looking above them. Understand that you are building a relationship of collegiality that is one of openness, truth, common sense, clarity of purpose, and gaining acceptance of a shared vision.

Of intrinsic value to any leader is their understanding of emotional intelligence and how it plays into your demonstration of leadership and approach to the inclusion of your team. "Emotional intelligence (EI) is the ability to perceive, interpret, demonstrate, control, evaluate, and use emotions to communicate with and relate to others effectively and constructively."[1] Awareness of your own personal skills and strengths, the ability to accept mistakes and move on by learning from them, handling emotions in difficult settings, and self-confidence in your abilities to manage a problem by understanding and being sensitive to the feelings of others — these are essential qualities. This discussion is built into the lessons learned that follow each section of the experience.

Finally, I like to use the term *leadership sleuthing* to define my baseline for driving my decision-making. Through my learned experience, I have found that you are forever building a foundation of understanding that offers opportunities for educated decision-making during critical moments — moments that can define your leadership legacy. Being known as someone who can listen to advice, take advice willingly, apply critical listening skills, understand the value of hearing from all sides of a topic, and strategically question to gain footing on decisions that impact people, budgets, taxes, rates, policies, labor, and key interest groups will be valuable for gaining consensus where leadership must be shown. I define these elements as

---

[1] By Kendra Cherry, Emotional Intelligence, VeryWell Mind, November 7, 2022.

sleuthing skills — skills that a person of solid moral and ethical values must demonstrate if they hope to succeed.

Prequel – The Early Years Which Defined My Core Ethical Line in the Sand

ATHENS, OHIO

I started early in experiencing this feeling that I was warming to a leading role when my Catholic grade school principal assigned me the responsibility of running the videotape system for movie days for all grades, 1st through 8th. I was an altar boy by then and a regular participant in early daily church services. I was also given the responsibility of delivering the bank deposits from church offerings received from daily services. This required me to leave school, walk half a mile downtown to the bank, get a receipt, and return the receipt to the principal within half an hour. No one else was offered that duty for several years. Being involved with Scouting during these years also offered skills development in outdoor activities that I have used throughout my life. My brother and I started as Explorer Scouts rather than following the standard scout profile, which required climbing the various ranks to achieve Eagle status, whereas Explorers only had to earn Eagle status. This allowed my brother and me, along with several other Explorers, to serve as mentors and guides for the other Scouts to experience all opportunities open to them, from camping, hiking, and exploring to merit badges, public speaking, volunteering, and more.

My confidence expanded when a group of friends in my 9th and 10th-grade public school classes developed a pickup game of soccer, which was not at that time a high school sport. I played as a forward and was a leading scorer for my side. Our group was approached by the local university soccer team, which wanted to have scrimmage matches as practice for their upcoming college games. Unexpectedly, we beat the college boys — to their dismay.

LAWRENCE, KANSAS

At this point, the family moved to another university town, where I completed high school and went on to college. I took the opportunity to act in three school plays in a leading role to build my confidence in speaking in front of a crowd — something that was slowly developing through my exposure as a high school debater. The latter was rough but necessary. Learning how to speak from the podium, in front of your peers, and in a logical and progressive step-by-step approach to arguing and justifying a position is an excellent learning experience. It benefits any and all debaters for the future, building confidence and practicing a tone of voice that engages your audience to listen. I grew from that experience and kept getting that lead role feeling.

When I turned 18 and became subject to the draft, my brother and I showed up at a bus station for delivery to a military facility for a medical assessment. The staff sergeant, out of the blue, assigned me as group leader, responsible for getting all twenty-five draftees to the medical facility, signing them in, ensuring they were fully processed, and returning them with a sign-off from the medical facility. I was successful.

There was a period following these successes when I felt out of the loop for leadership opportunities. Working at the local McDonald's never generated an opportunity to grow into a lead manager role, even though my brother was given that opportunity several times. My undergraduate years at the University of Kansas were a blur and unremarkable, except for taking summer classes in literature in Barcelona, Spain, which allowed me to see and experience Europe while living on an average of $10 a day. The dollar was strong in those years. I graduated with a 3.2 GPA in history and political science without a real plan for the future. This led to working in construction for one year. From that experience, I learned that I was not going to accept a low wage for the rest of my life, so I jumped into graduate school for urban planning at Kansas State University.

Getting into the program was my first experience selling myself as a capable, committed, and willing student who had what it took to complete the coursework successfully. The dean offered me a semester to prove myself, and that is what I did. I blossomed during those four years, earning a 4.0 GPA while taking on leadership roles, including serving as the first president of the Student Planning Association, finance chair of the Graduate Student Council, and later president of the Graduate Student Council.

In the latter leadership role, I learned early that funds available for graduate programs for master's and Ph.D. students were never drawn heavily from annual budgets provided through tuition. With this understanding, I pushed and gained full funding for planning students to attend annual professional conferences for development and mentoring. I also started what became a strength of my professional career: the value of efficiency, understanding budget availability, remedying roadblocks in administrative activities, not asking for approval to act until a solution was fully defined, visualizing what I wanted to achieve and what it would take to achieve it, and never complaining if it took longer than planned. This began when I pushed, without asking, for the creation of a Graduate Student Handbook. I had a team prepare and submit a draft to the Graduate School. They were surprised and exhilarated by the document and fully funded the printing and distribution to all future graduate degree applicants—something that continues to this day.

On top of all this, I had taken on the challenge of a master's dissertation based on the success of the Space Shuttle program. I wrote on the subject of *A Multi-Disciplinary Approach to an Outer Space Community.* My thesis committee offered no advice on how I should approach writing on this subject. This was an early precursor to the budget initiatives I would later write to initiate a new direction for an organization I was leading. More on this subject later.

The dissertation committee's professional connections were invaluable in rounding out my research requirements. For example, my Chairman was in the Navy Reserves and provided access to confined space research experiments, where test facilities were located underwater. The test subjects were required to spend months at a time in a confined space to assess the potential to create cooperative psychological work/life balance conditions for extended mission assignments. A second professor had been involved with the training of the original chimpanzees that went to space before human flight. He provided access to contacts he had at the NASA Johnson Space Center in Houston, TX, where I interviewed four astronauts for their perspectives on my topic area. The last member of my committee was one of the lighting design engineers on the lunar landing module sent to the Moon. He provided suggestions on the types of material, wiring, piping, shielding, atmospheric systems, and so on that would be required.

The topic required the formulation of an international planning policy for the various nation-states that had space aspirations. I had identified countries that would make use of an international space station primarily for security purposes and surveillance opportunities, in addition to the obvious laboratory research and commercial development interests a space station might offer. Ultimately, the final submittal, five years later, turned out to be a success, with my orals gaining approval. Interestingly, they were all surprised by its recommendation. Essentially, I had defined a comprehensive scheme for implementing a space station program that required:

1. A multinational beginning—no single country could afford to implement such a program by itself.

2. The eventual incorporation of private sector commercial development interests and private funding for long-term investment purposes, ensuring eventual economic returns and reducing public funding commitments when private economic interests began driving technological improvements.

3. The need for a military-type organizational framework on the station, involving both military and civilian interests, to ensure a

leadership alignment existed to centralize and establish a decision structure to manage and handle all environmental conditions, standard operations, or emergencies.

4. A demonstration of the capability of governments, research interests, the military, and diverse male and female specialists to succeed and build a reputation that space is the next logical frontier to develop.

The success of the current international space station demonstrates everything I envisioned before it became a goal for NASA and other national interests.

What comes next are my life experiences that define my professional work years. Those experiences built and designed my leadership standing, which I perceived as desirable yet reluctant examples of engagement. Interestingly, I was approached more often and asked to serve in leadership roles rather than outright applying for them. My bottom line, in many ways, was to be an example of the best available talent, intent on raising the bar on outcomes where I could contribute. The priority was public benefit over private or political interests. It was also my desire to earn opportunities through solid professional capabilities, which I continued to learn and improve upon throughout my career.

I will also argue — where others may not agree — that stepping into a leadership role (i.e., assistant city manager, deputy director, deputy human resources manager, and so on) right out of graduate school does not provide the kind of foundational training for leadership that I believe is needed. It is my learned belief that a new person does not have:

- Exposure at a staff level to appreciate the nuances of departmental staff pressures.

- An understanding of the lack of adequate funding to implement a program effectively.

- Experience in learning how to work with peers without any authority.

- Practice in learning to justify new funding needs.

- Knowledge of how to build new or revised policy documents.

- Exposure to learning how to build capacity to analyze operating conditions in the office and the field.

- Adequate practice honing analytical and research skills to learn how to write and argue facts, and so on.

It is not unusual for good budgeteers to become the mentor or go-to source for ideas from a department staffer who is under pressure to help expand or implement a new program with little information to build a solid funding request. This is the key training program for constructive leadership in any organization you may pursue to lead.

Leaders who can pull their lower-level staff experience into a senior leadership role will have a better understanding of the limitations faced in gaining new ground, where the minefield is littered with conditions they have learned to avoid. The budget office is one of those key points of influence where you learn more about your assigned departments than the departments themselves, giving you an edge in driving change where roadblocks have existed for years.

Please keep in mind that the discussion of specific locales and places of employment is more than five years old at the latest example, such that changes may or may not be reflected as reality today due to changes that have been implemented, resolved, and pursued based on new leadership and fresh perspectives that I have not had control over, nor could I influence, since I have been distant from my days of involvement. Please look at these examples of my work history, telling of the conditions and situations of historical circumstances that have potentially led to improvements but in no way establish blame on any person or individual unnamed in this historical account. My hope is that you can learn from my experience — notable or not—how to manage, handle, and drive change for the benefit of the governmental organization and the public it serves.

William B. Gilmore.

The Role of a Leadership Sleuth Begins in the Trenches

ONE OF THE MID-WEST PLAINS STATES
Agency Description:

The State Legislature legislatively authorized the governor's Office to have a research and planning office under its direct control as an opportunity to:

a) Prepare new policy initiatives,

b) Approach other states to learn from, coordinate, or assess a proposal pursuing a change on a specific issue,

c) Guide federal funding distribution and administrative development and rollout,

d) Represent the governor's office at national, state, and local levels,

e) Evaluate the impact of new initiatives in advance of public notification,

f) Build consensus around a long-term planning strategy with one or more state agencies, and so on.

My professional work life began as an internship for a State Planning and Research Division under the Department of Administration, an arm of the Governor's Office in this Midwestern state. State agencies had never done long-term planning per se. They thought in four-year increments, and our role was to help them develop a twenty-year planning vision. I also managed the distribution of federal funds to county planning agencies, built from their annual submittals for multi-year plans that demonstrated realism, coordination with local governments, and solid examples of long-term land use plans that aligned with private sector growth opportunities. There were also opportunities to assist with writing a governor's speech on a variety of subjects. This led to my serving as the governor's representative to the State League of Municipalities. The mentoring I received from the Planning Office was foundational for me in learning how to write, analyze, and think on topics of broad interest that fit within political realities.

I also learned the reality of being political fodder when the State Legislature terminated our division by defunding it — having been too effective — and shifting the funding to procure a new computer system. The conservative-leaning Legislature felt the Democratic Governor was too effective in his messaging, blaming that on our agency, to the dismay and roadblock of a solid conservative majority who could not limit the governor's progress on several major topics.

My newfound freedom led me back home to the reality that I had never truly learned how to run an organization of any size during my time in urban planning. As a result, I enrolled in a master's program for Public Administration at the University of Kansas. For the second time, I found myself needing to sell my capability to succeed in the program, and again, I was given a semester to prove myself — which I did. It was clear upon graduation that a majority of graduate professors should be experienced in their subject matter, having been in the field as organizational division heads or city managers working through scenarios that stretched their foundational thinking from college to real-life experiences. However, there were a few professors who rolled into teaching slots right out of graduate school and did not have exposure to real conditions in the field. As a result, their opinions on a variety of subjects lacked standing, foundation, and the ability to push back sagely on questions from individuals who had been out in the public arena. Basically, they lacked exposure to the irregularities of poor managers, poor policy protocols, poor coordination, poor hiring policies, poor planning, poor budgeting, and ultimately poor leadership qualities.

Getting along with all of my professors was a challenge. In one case, after receiving a poor grade, I had to take an additional class to offset the mistake of challenging an unremarkable professor. That additional class, *How to Prepare a Ph.D. Proposal* turned out to be foundational for me. I used the Ph.D. proposal format as a standard guideline for preparing all of my future analytical work in every role I was in — to justify proposed arguments for new funding, new programming, new policy modification or generation, creating capital reserves, amending utility rate structures, and so on.

At the time of graduation, an offer from a legislative office came through, which I chose to acknowledge. The department head knew of the termination from the State Planning Office, which happened for no reason other than political expediency. The intent was to build on my experience with the state legislative process and push me into understanding state priorities through a legislative budget fiscal office.

William B. Gilmore.

Midwest Plains State

State Agency Description:

State Legislatures employ Legislative Research Departments to help legislators — House and Senate — with research on topics of interest, conducting fiscal audits to confirm funding demands, writing draft language for committee review and discussion, serving as staffing aides to legislative committees, and writing legislation for eventual confirmation or failure. They generally include a fiscal section responsible for monitoring each state agency's spending, financial demands, policy requirements, site audits, and federal regulatory requirements. They are determinedly nonpartisan and are built on providing honest, robust, clearly outlined research for a learned approach to decision-making.

After graduating with my second master's degree, I went back to state government, working for the State Legislative Research Department's Fiscal Section. The work involved preparing a legislative budget response to the governor's Office of Management and Budget deliverable as a negotiating strategy for annual spending protocols. Sleuthing through my assigned state agencies focused on their facilities in the field and evaluating budget priorities. The work included qualifying explanations of funding needs to the realities of regulation, expectation, strategic decision-making, changing conditions, political realities, and authorized oversights—which rarely came to light—were the challenges of the day. Staffing the House and Senate Ways and Means Committees was also eye-opening. It wasn't unusual for legislators to hang themselves out to dry and need to be reeled in by staff to save them from a bit of humiliation. This required staff to step in and pull the subject back to a more logical and reasonable dimension, defining the vision the legislator was trying to convey. Let's just say that it could be challenging to meet that goal. The primary value of this experience was that you had to have the confidence to stand up, speak clearly, and carry the message of the legislator to a favorable outcome before a sea of legislators. This was training by fire and required being on your game every day. Our division, as a group, thrived in this environment and played the long game because the shifting foundation of politicians who ran for office frequently lived and died on our data.

Suffering burnout from two years of 14-hour days performing legislative work—with summers spent researching the next season's political priorities—I left, telling my team and Ways and Means Committee members that they had regularly, consistently, and deliberately underfunded a state program operating under federal guidelines. The recommendation offered was to set aside a reserve fund to pay a potential fine and to establish new funding to meet expanded service requirements under both federal and state guidelines. They denied my recommendation. A year after my departure, the woman who took my place called and informed me that they were fined and forced to budget to the amount I had recommended.

Lessons Learned From State Government:

Politicians come with many stripes, and the first rule is to find out what degree of moral compass they follow. Do they have a realistic perspective of the world? Are they party-driven or value-driven? Will they accept analysis to make decisions, or are they willing to ignore facts to achieve political fiction? And finally, does the public interest compete against personal gain? If you stay in the game after answering these questions, at least you know how high the bar is for you to have any influence over policy or procedure. You also must know that building relationships with key individuals who publicly display staunch positions on many subjects can also be open to amending their position to adjust issues that undermine their stance and potentially the confidence of their funding entities and voters. Staff learn to be, in many ways, the fluid that allows solid objects to readjust to ease the pressure and tension of recalcitrant forces as we carry the message or intel that serves to blunt a stuck position.

Sleuthing skills, when involved in public employment, require a degree of inquisitiveness that must be endorsed, encouraged, understood, communicated among your peers, promoted financially and professionally, and have the full backing of your leader(s). Sleuthing skills are also a critical piece of the foundation that makes for visionary, realistic, forward-looking, and risk-taking traits. These skills will find you standing out negatively to the narcissistic, narrow-minded pool of division managers and community leaders that make up many of our weak governmental leadership teams. Why? Because you can demonstrate your findings both factually and logically. Basically, you have waited to make your play for new efficiencies. You have outlined a budget remedy for adequate funding, proposed a policy amendment to correct protocols, and suggested a leadership modification to address a weakness due to the poor condition of existing standards within the organization.

Innate character benefits include having a thick skin, confidence in a position based on solid research and examples of program application, a calm demeanor during a presentation before a menacing set of department heads, an openness to risk that is counter to existing perspectives, and a clear explanation of long-term budget savings with the necessary short-term investment requirement(s). A successful conclusion makes for an exciting and potentially satisfying outcome. Ultimately, this experience builds your skills catalog, offering a threat to power, anticipating and accepting the consequences of disclosing shortcomings by leadership, developing your strategic value, strengthening the power of your voice and respect for your professionalism, and adding to your resume for your future.

The reality that exists in a legislative sphere is who wields control, subtle or demonstrative. Legislative staff can remain relatively independent, but avoiding chances to gather influence to gain support for an ethically responsible position can break your confidence and may numb you to avoid pushing against the obvious limitations of clear research when the wall of political opinion is against you. This is when a legislative staff person must decide if there is a purpose to remain or if there is a chance of attaining a better outcome. It generally depends on whether there is a chance of a change in the ruling power. This decision is also affected by understanding whether there was an adequate demonstration of support for your proposal.

A MIDWEST CITY
Local Agency Description:

This local government was run using an elected body with an elected Mayor, who hires their senior executive to administer local governmental services for the benefit of the community, paid for through a tax, fee, and grant structure. Local government is a strange and interesting animal with many different stripes of political persuasion, self-interest, naïve perspectives, and risk avoidance. Somehow, accepting that the elected body is smart, dedicated, and interested in good government—which is rare—as are its professionals, must be determined separately for each local entity you may work for. In many cases, electors focus on getting reelected over the solid success of government institutions.

The breakout moment for broadening my leadership skills, using my sleuthing traits extensively, was the moment I began working for local government following my time with state government. One of my principal mentors, who was head of the Budget Division, told me the reality that I was walking into. Basically, he had recently been faced with a challenge involving a corrupt politician who managed city accounts. My mentor was told to transfer funds to a certain bank for their illegal plans, where he was faced with a gun on the table, threatening mayhem to his future health. My mentor refused and walked out, which led to the corrupt politician being found impaled on a statue near City Hall the next day, with the assumption being he couldn't meet his required payment obligations. It was at that point he asked if I was still interested. I assured him I was, and over the next four years, he had my back and gave me the freedom to sleuth out fiscal and programmatic problems.

Looking briefly ahead at my professional development, it has been my experience that it is a rare practice for budget division staff to get out of their chairs to visit the field where the departments they oversee actually work, operate, and implement their assigned tasks. This leaves the budget analyst in the position of conjecturing, posturing, and imagining their argument for funding practicality based on uncertain and unseen activities. The findings could demonstrate inadequate funding, improper focus, the wrong equipment or tools to do the job well, and reliance on conjecture and trust of department staff to be honest about their departmental needs and realities — which is anathema to any confident sleuther. This can lead to excess funding and wasting critical dollars better used for other needs. That was never my problem as a developing budget analyst (sleuth), who found it both threatening and informative to visit the field and inform one of my departments each year that I would be targeting extra effort on a particular budget area.

The first time I pushed this extra effort initiative was at the adoption of the first city budget, where I had identified specific irregularities in several departmental activities. At the City Administrator's meeting with his department heads, my mentor aired my findings and forewarned the Public Works Department that one of his staff would be doing in-the-field research to clarify and potentially correct a problem he felt existed with the city's Public Golf Course. He left it undefined at that time but did state that my assumption was that public golf courses, if run effectively, generally were profitable after three or four years. The current golf course was underwater financially after seven years, yet the course, by all measures used to date, showed it should be profitable. The department head wished my mentor good luck and brushed it aside.

My mentor said it was a go, even though the City Administrator told him to limit my time-wasting effort on something he didn't believe had merit. Even though I had five other departments under my purview as a Budget Analyst and was central to the development of a new multi-year capital improvement program, I spent the next year, until the next budget submittal, working on my fiscal analysis of the golf course. The fieldwork was invaluable to building my cash flow argument because I would show up randomly on various days of the week to count the number of baskets of balls used at each hour of the day, the number of golf carts in play, the number of players in play, the amount of inventory sold through the pro shop, the number of pro golf classes offered by the golf pro, and what the books actually showed. My findings proved that the golf course was indeed profitable, and a sizeable percentage was missing. The golf pro was benefiting substantially from a contract that gave him all the profits from his classes, which was legitimate, but also half the profits from the golf carts, golf ball baskets, and the clubhouse inventory of sales.

Comparing contracts with other courses, out-of-state and in-state, this was not the standard agreement. Having worked for state government and acquired a few friendly contacts, I was able to gain access to a search of area banks through a complaint I filed with the Secretary of State and the State Attorney General. What they found was that the golf pro had a bank account in which he deposited regular funds, but others used who were associated with one of the county's political parties. Essentially, the golf course served as a funding source for area politics that guaranteed one of the key primary counties and election districts in the state would provide support for those aligned with the protocols of that political party.

The outcome had me rewriting the golf pro's contract, transferring profits sent to the political party's account back into the city's coffers, recommending new reporting requirements for all political entities, revising reporting protocols, and adding more funding to capital needs that had been delayed due to a lack of funding. The state handled any criminal and civil complaints that came out of it. It also put the City Administrator and City Engineer on notice that their management of and knowledge of this illegal scheme would be kept secure in a report undelivered to the Mayor and Council and would be used as leverage to improve their willingness to correct behavior in their departments.

The success of the Golf Course findings led me to recommend an evaluation and changes to the Right of Way Division of Public Works. I was forewarned to be careful by several department heads who had been impacted by the outcome of the loss of party funding and their roles in it. The warning was due to the scuttlebutt I had found that the Right of Way (ROW) Agent was the key personality running and guaranteeing election outcomes for years, going back to when graves were voters. This latter piece was no longer a problem but gave a flavor of the degree of influence held by this particular person. My research found that the ROW Agent had been instrumental in gaining the alignment of properties for the siting of the interstate highway system that ran through the metropolitan area, handling millions of dollars in federal funds. That program was fast running down since there was little to no work being done on land procurement in the last fifteen years. Hence, my interest in why he was still in his historical capacity. I looked at and obtained the state's guidelines for ROW administration, as well as other area state programs, to compare the city's guidelines. Significant changes were needed to bring the old language up to state standards, which had been largely ignored and allowed too much freedom for the ROW Agent.

With those revisions in hand, I arranged a meeting with the ROW Agent, and to my surprise, his two principal lieutenants — lawyers by trade — were the last two individuals I expected to see working with him. But in keeping with the scuttlebutt I had started with, I should not have been surprised because it was a requirement of the ROW Agent that any political individual who wanted to be successful in that county and/or that part of the state had to essentially kiss his ring to guarantee the vote. Candidates for Governor had been doing it for years, attending on-site meetings to gain his support. The two lawyers, it turned out, were the President of the State Senate and the Speaker of the House. I knew them personally from my time at Legislative Research, working on the Ways and Means Committees. After surprising the ROW Agent with my familiarity with those two esteemed individuals, they reviewed my materials. They stated emphatically that the ROW Agent needed to consider retirement, which was my recommendation based on my reputation as a fiscal sleuth and my findings on the office's administrative policies and procedures. I avoided any alignment with the earlier financial problem since funding plans for future political activities had been substantially disrupted, and all three of them were effectively impacted by the loss of access to those dollars.

Next was my evaluation of the Parking Control Division within the Facilities Management Department. The division head was Black, female, and an elected member of county government — a significant alignment that assured access to a voting bloc of citizens and coordinated influence with county programs through her local appointment. Again, the division operated underwater after being expanded with new parking structures and staff. Field tests of Parking Control operations were extremely telling. To be brief, the findings on this division showed the division head stealing cash, failing to establish clear accounting and reporting guidelines aligned with requirements from cash booth activities (matching tickets to payments), a lack of documentation to create a daily vehicle count of parking structure users, and no bonding requirements for cash managers in the office to ensure accountability to a municipal code of conduct.

Going around the City Administrator, who would not fire a member of the County Council, I went to the Mayor, who proceeded to report and gain her termination — briefly — until the City Administrator made a major play to gain the support of the rest of the Council to reverse their decision and reengage her based on her value to the political requirements of the city and county. Despite the City Administrator's desire to fire me for insubordination, I pushed back and begged him to fire me so that I could take my detailed reports and the council's actions to the press. He relented and agreed to my demands to revise the operations of the Parking Control office so that the division transitioned to a profitable position for the first time since its founding.

This episode introduces the problem of many local and city councils, which are elected to oversee the operations, contracts, expenditures, policies, and procedures implemented through the CityAdministrator'sManager's Office. Clarity of activity below the committee level can be blunted by a failure to provide suitable examples of benchmarks, strategic timing of progress against planned schedules, poorly defined programs and their missions, undefined goals and objectives, and department heads who deliberately cloud their message because they neither understand nor have the capacity to create a viable program initiative. This is not the case in every locale or city across the country, but it is more frequent than not. It is also important to understand that some councils have been deliberate in their obtrusiveness because they don't necessarily like or are open to change that may shift the balance of power out of their control. The reason is that it gives them the leverage to be the white knights and saviors of the public purse, whereas, in reality, the Council may have hired a pliant and weak-willed holder of the manager's Office who is willing to wait to be told what the mission is rather than being an independent voice challenging his own staff to be leaders in their departments and to be efficient and effective in their delivery of public services. This happens too often to dismiss it as hearsay.

I also had the opportunity to develop an early example of an asset management program well before it became a central endeavor for public organizations and their extensive infrastructure systems. The Capital Budget became a separate document, distinct from the Annual Budget, because of the importance of long-term financial planning. The intent was to focus on renewal and replacement requirements of critical assets, setting benchmarks for service delivery, and developing tracking systems to monitor trends in condition, failure, reliability, criticality, and service delivery in order to prioritize maintenance of existing systems over new asset additions. Each department had to submit annual spending requests and participate in a committee evaluation that listed a set of categories, highest to lowest priority, to assist with evaluating and justifying the importance of a specific request. The rating system emphasized maintenance over new asset additions.

With this new procedure for selecting capital spending needs, the write-ups justifying spending requirements improved dramatically and required site visits by committee members to ensure the visual assessments matched the descriptions of condition and criticality. It was interesting to watch engineering and facilities management representatives attempt to influence the scoring to push funding for their internal priorities, which required my memory of historical spending justifications from prior years that did not match their history of spending nor tie directly to a policy initiative that was never established.

As I said earlier, leadership skills development isn't always safe from ethical challenges, such that risk-taking must be measured and used strategically to leave you on the safe side of a major catastrophe that could affect your professional development for the long term. I knew that my chance for higher office with my current employer was out of the question because of my deliberate undermining of Authority and chain-of-command protocols. This was clearly stated to me by the city administrator, who was the city's former chief financial officer. This latter position was vacant, and at the conclusion of the interview with him, he stated that I would not be selected since I was not willing to be part of the team that turned a blind eye to the inefficiencies his group allowed. Instead, he appointed a younger individual with some narcissistic tendencies that mirrored the general leaning of the ruling members. This was despite my efforts to effectively reverse years of financial losses to the tune of several million dollars and to effectively reduce the pressure to raise property taxes. The budget team also received the Government Finance Officer's Association award for the Operating and Capital Budget documents we produced three years running. Remember the old adage, "No good deed goes unpunished." The only recourse was relocation.

While searching for the next new thing, I had the opportunity to come together with two other young professionals going through their early break-in years in local government from around the metropolitan area. The three of us chose to push the formation of a group known as the Young Professionals Forum that would provide mentoring, introductions, and cross-communication of professional duties facing young professionals clearly wanting to engage with senior leadership to develop and broaden their governmental opportunities in the field of County, City, Non-Profit, Utility, and Regional Planning entities. Somehow, I was asked to take the lead in this new forum, and over the next year, I established a monthly speaker's bureau that rotated through each community where young professional participants came from. I received several kudos for the speakers, lunch venues, and topics that allowed for interaction on topics current and in the news, affecting everyone differently. The city manager of a large neighboring city commented during his participation as the guest of honor that he was very glad there was a group like this. He said he wished there had been one available when he was starting in this profession.

Lessons Learned From Local Government:

Older communities, considered the poor sister to the larger metropolitan area, are more likely than not to demonstrate a poor management philosophy that pursues personal gain for the connected few in leadership at the expense of weak and unassuming staff appointments. Findings show that weak appointments won't challenge the status quo, regardless of how badly it reflects on all involved. Gaining access through appointments to a budget office offers opportunities to learn about the deep fissures that may exist in all departments by asking the right questions, conducting field research, and demonstrating small gains in improvement from those findings while beginning to open the door to ideas that start to crack the status quo of past conduct. Change for the sake of change is not your goal. Changing work culture and exposing bad conduct to the light of day is your goal. Telling your revisionist story through budget deliberations that paint a different picture from the folklore promoted by embedded leadership is best done in a public setting that involves progressive interests who listen for opportunities to push for change. Many of you have heard the old adage, "We've always done it this way." Personally, anyone who states that phrase in my presence is put on a very short leash, demoted from lead roles, and given a very negative performance assessment until they categorically demonstrate a new personal philosophy — one that embraces positive change and improving the quality of service delivery as the vision and mantra of their office and role.

Gaining access to council members who are progressive and potential drivers of change can be difficult for a staff analyst to develop without authorization from senior leadership. As a result, being hired by a department and/or division head who has an independent streak, is open to a little risk-taking, and may have already developed an opening with a member of the Council offers a chance to introduce new directions and initiatives. If the right set of questions and expected answers can be fed into a council committee discussion, it can then push for new movement and additional research. Essentially, the division head has identified a champion in the ruling body who wants to help pave the way for new initiatives to take root. Gaining access to this champion — who can be prepared for committee and/or council discussion in advance of the meeting — can go a long way in warming the message to a new set of considerations that may give change a chance to proceed. In this local government, it wasn't unusual for budget staff to be invited to the after-council-meeting saloon to share stories, discuss meeting outcomes, open the door to new initiatives, and build trust with council members who were reluctant parties to the power brokers running city politics.

Every staff analyst must determine for themselves what ethical and moral avenue they will follow over the course of their professional career. I could have chosen to follow a road that waits for direction and guidance from leadership, avoiding clarity to protect political interests over public interests. But I chose to put the public before politics; efficiency over outdated methods, new opportunities over historical steadfastness, a short-term bump in spending to achieve long-term savings through technology that can reduce labor costs, and hiring better-trained staff who are more capable and embrace a challenging work ethic. Ultimately, the target is to build a budget document that serves to define a roadmap for growth and balanced development by highlighting a realistic vision of the future, goals and objectives that lay out the plans for progress, and metrics that measure progress over time. I also chose to drive change based on professional conference participation, research on topics that benefit community capacities, and being a risk-taker at the forefront of the next new thing where assessment suggested a real public benefit.

Life in the public governmental environment is challenging for anyone. In many cases, you are putting your ethical and moral nature before profitable opportunities in the private sector. Public sector pay is not commensurate with the level of exposure you experience in public sector roles. This can be frustrating in many ways, but it is also stimulating if you can overcome roadblocks to change. That level of satisfaction has its own value. Ultimately, the skills you gain in the public sector will give you more experience in opening doors to new opportunities — if you push to improve the organization you are in, demonstrating useful capabilities that will define your resume.

William B. Gilmore.

Leadership Where Good Deeds Can Be Both Praised and Punished

A MID-ATLANTIC COMMUNITY ON THE EAST COAST

Agency Description:

A Municipal Utility Authority (MUA) is a creature of the state legislature that allows a governmental entity to be formed for the purpose of specific services authorized by statute, in this case, water and sewer services. They have full Authority to establish rates, authorize long-term debt, and authorize contracts for service support without the approval of the local government. The intent is to operate outside of the political environment associated with local government, which allows the utility to make spending decisions regardless of local governmental challenges. The primary point of influence by the local government is with the appointment of new board members, who may or may not be sycophants of the Mayor or Council. Independence to make significant decisions that may impact rates, debt, and service levels is the purpose and benefit of having an independent MUA with appointed members from banking, business, regulatory agencies, and education, to name a few — individuals who prioritize ratepayers over politics.

My relocation to the East Coast was expensive for me in many ways. Regardless of the cost of the move, I left behind connections, professional relationships, the comfort of knowing the larger metropolitan environment and state legislative activities, and partnerships with other community interests that provided a baseline of operational awareness — key to gaining access and progress in many local governmental initiatives. I was heading into an entirely new environment focused on municipal water and wastewater services that were independent of the immediate control of the local government. But the leadership opportunity for me as Deputy Manager of a utility authority in a relatively small community of 29,000 residents and 27 square miles — when I had previously worked with statewide influence and a large municipal entity of 640 square miles — turned out to be a game-changer that offered expansive development advantages.

The Utility Board had never seen someone with my training and drive for improvement. Their experience with senior management, including the present individual in charge, was with someone desirous of being seen as in charge but who lacked personality, openness to advice, and serious experience with writing position papers on policy and budget initiatives — though they did have a sound perspective on key points of control and capital project oversight. These latter examples included the replacement of the primary and secondary wastewater treatment units with a new tertiary process train that would be used to provide sludge irrigation to the 200 acres of farmland surrounding the treatment facilities. We recommended that, during the construction of the new facilities, the utility delay authorizing connection permits for sewer treatment to new residential/commercial development projects as a new impact fee program was being prepared in conjunction with the utility's engineering and legal consultants. The outcome would ultimately provide full funding for new capital requirements associated with growth, removing the obligation for funding from existing ratepayers.

As a result of these very positive initiatives, within six months of being in my Deputy role, the Board moved to have me assigned as Executive Director, with my former boss newly titled Manager of Development. The Utility Board was very progressive and desired real leadership, which they did not see in the sitting General Manager. This promotion was built upon my preparation of an annual budget submittal along with a new multi-year capital improvement program that incorporated the new impact fee funding strategy, as discussed above, to expand the utility to meet explosive growth following the recent conclusion of a sewer moratorium. This moratorium had been imposed to allow for an upgrade of the treatment facility to a tertiary advanced biological treatment process. Again, the key message about impact fees is that development pays the full cost of development impacts on utility services.

Of interest to local government managers was the attempt by the local Mayor to have the utility incorporate local government infrastructure requirements affected by development into our impact fee program. The problem with this intrusion by the Mayor was:

a) The city had already approved, through their planning board, most developer permit submittals issued during the moratorium, closing the door to amending those permits to charge for infrastructure improvements at the developer's expense, whereas the utility had held back its permit approval pending completion of the treatment plant expansion.

b) State law regarding Municipal Utility Authorities (MUAs) did not allow for coordinated activities with local governments because MUAs were independent, self-funding, and could obligate the rate base to long-term debt without council approval. In addition, there was no attempt to initiate an inter-local service agreement, which might have allowed for coordination.

c) The Mayor threatened to stack the utility board with her appointees, who would follow her lead.

D) The Mayor knew this request was illegal, that developers would sue for this action, and — being an attorney — demonstrated a low ethical, legal standard.

Nevertheless, the budget I introduced for the MUA met the qualifications recommended by the Government Finance Officers Association (GFOA) for an award, having won that certification the prior three years with my former employer. Additionally, I prepared a new rate structure for water and sewer services, led community public hearings to gain approval, and secured the Board's adoption. The proposed Capital Maintenance Budget provided a five-year spending strategy that matched development requirements with an emphasis on preventive maintenance of existing facilities. Impact fee payments provided cash to install all necessary infrastructure, allowing the Utility to avoid issuing new long-term debt. We also paid down existing long-term debt and incorporated a new maintenance reserve requirement to be funded annually in support of planned repair and rehabilitation of existing assets.

The negative message to the public with the new rate structure was a doubling of the base rate, with a multiplier driven by consumption. However, the positive message was that impact fees from the development community would ultimately reverse the increased base rate over a period of five years. This would be achieved through the creation of maintenance reserves, implementation of a multi-year preventive maintenance strategy, the addition of new customer accounts, avoidance of long-term debt for capital expansion and repairs, and the introduction of new technology and efficiency initiatives to offset labor requirements.

The success of this campaign was palpable and led to the local government asking me to serve in an interim capacity as Township Manager along with my role as Executive Director of the Utility as they proceeded with the hiring of a replacement Township Manager. This happened at the same time the International Water Association approved my topic for presentation at the Osaka International Water Conference, which was to demonstrate the ability of small utilities to be as effective as, or even more effective than, larger private utilities around the world in strategic service delivery. I had been assigned to a session comparing the privately run Anglican Water Company of England to my independent local governmental MUA. The session was effective in storyboarding my public sector success and control of rates in contrast to a very corporate investor approach that incorporated a profit incentive, whereas my MUA used savings (our profit) to reinvest in our utility.

The current anointed Mayor, chosen from the elected council members each new year, was familiar with my progressive work at the Utility and was strongly aligned with the Chairman of the Utility. The Township Council had been frustrated by the poor performance of the prior Township Manager, whom they terminated, and they needed someone to step in during the interim before the next new Township Council was elected to appoint a new Manager. The Council took direction from the Mayor and assigned me to the role. However, I had made it clear that I was not someone to wait for and be a placeholder to maintain the status quo. I planned to make changes along with the support of the various department heads. I vocalized this at my first department head meeting, where I challenged them to keep up with my plans to introduce change, new technology, new policy guidelines, and an open-door policy that I expected them all to take advantage of. It was well received, given the past history of an unwillingness to listen and act on their concerns.

It was very clear from the scuttlebutt provided by many of the township employees that, historically, the Township Council chose managers they could control and who would drive project initiatives they perceived as viable for the community, regardless of what a professional manager with progressive objectives would do. My philosophy put administrative efficiency as a first priority before new program startups where there wasn't in-house training or knowledge capacity to establish a viable new program. A driver of change was needed and clearly lacking, given that history showed a placeholder was regularly selected — someone who wouldn't cause a problem for their political interests and focused on getting them reelected.

I hit the ground running from the first Council meeting when I was formally appointed to the interim role. They first asked for a plan to clean up the three shopping center parking areas and to have it ready by the next meeting, which was in one week. I stated that they didn't need a plan but action to get it done. They voted for a plan. I chose to act, going against the adopted Council motion. The next day, I called each shopping center owner along with my Public Works Manager and agreed on a plan of action. By the end of the following day, the parking lots were cleaned up, new paint was initiated for improved parking alignments, new decorative trash bins were distributed, and the Township agreed to more frequent pickups of trash containment without an increase in service fees. The letter I prepared for the Council described the outcome and forward-looking agreement, but the Mayor still asked for the plan. Instead, I turned to the three owners who came to the meeting and asked them to comment. They stated emphatically that I should be appointed as the permanent manager because I was the first manager ever to understand the requirements of business and that they could work with me collegially without undue pressure.

This experience represents one of those times when action—while ignoring the Council—resulted in a significantly positive outcome, based on a willingness to accept criticism for the larger benefit of the public and the need to make the best use of resources where demands for services regularly outstripped the capacities of the budgeted programs. My action set the tone for the remainder of my term, and the Council subsequently ended its practice of asking for a variety of initiatives. Instead, I took the lead, submitting multiple requests at each Council meeting for game-changing program adjustments, which included:

- A new financial management system,

- A new shared health plan for unionized and non-unionized employees,

- A new program of performance metrics to justify budget requests,

- A new joint community proposal for one-armed bandit trash pickup service that would reduce labor needs from three to one person and save on workman's compensation claims and insurance charges,

- The procurement of a new data management system to eliminate excessive buildup of boxed historical files for long-term data storage on laser disks,

- The automation of the township's phone system to eliminate a dedicated person for that task and

- The formation of a new budget process and capital request methodology.

All of this was accomplished using the practice of "management by walking around" and listening to staff concerns that made their work less than satisfying. The contract attorney to the Township Council was astonished at the work I was doing compared to the other fifteen communities he served in the same capacity. The proposal documents and fiscal notes I wrote were by far more comprehensive and descriptive of the initiatives being proposed than he had seen by other Managers. He stated that none of them were driving the amount of work I regularly pushed through my Council. I was able to complete all this work within nine months when the new Manager was appointed.

This latter comment by the attorney was informative and provided a bit of dismay for me. Why was what I was doing so out of the normal that he would make that type of comment? It is my fear that other managers fail to make clear at the time of appointment that they are their own evaluator of their performance, more so than the Council, and that I planned to move faster than they did on clearing out conditions that undermined efficiency, disrupted lines of communication and coordination, wasted budget and labor investment, failed to focus clearly on service delivery due to a lack of clearly defined protocols, and failure by department managers to make decisions when needed due to a sense of not having clear support and backing to act on their own, and so on.

This is where my prior experience in the budget office in state and local government paid off. The township division heads were dismayed when I left to return to the Utility because they hadn't had a real manager for over twenty years. They were very impressed when I had to have the pending mayor-elect escorted out of my office because of their unwillingness to follow normal protocol, sign in with my executive secretary, and give me the courtesy to complete what I was doing on the new budget report for the upcoming year. They couldn't believe I had the wherewithal to put the arrogant mayor-elect in their place. The last manager was known to waste his days playing computer games until tasked with a Council request. The next manager following me was a former detective with the local police force who I knew to be suitably weak-minded, had no training in professional management, and was easily led by the new Mayor, which was the reason for the appointment.

The staff understood why I couldn't stay. The newly appointed Mayor from the recent election and I did not see eye to eye on who really ran the Township. Legislatively, the manager had all the Authority. The Mayor's position was only ceremonial, but with collusion and a lack of backbone among other Council members, they followed the Mayor's lead regardless of the circumstances. The manager's position would have been compromised to consolidate power in the Mayor's hands. The new Mayor immediately chose to trash my budget document, which I had prepared for the new Council and met the guidelines of the Government Finance Officers Association, to restart the budget creation process in a less robust and less definitive manner. This allowed the message, which lacked clarity, to be controlled by the new Mayor for their narrow and less progressive service delivery.

Back in the executive director's saddle at the utility, a problem had developed: the administrative staff was in open conflict, disrupting customer service response activities, data development, financial reporting, procurement delays, and other issues. The root cause was the operator of the financial system, who, while sitting alone in her office, slowed reporting of budget status to demonstrate her importance over others who were her senior. I remembered what my old mentor had done when faced with a staff person in his budget office who regularly slept in his office. He was the son of a Council person and, therefore, couldn't be touched. So, he had the walls of his office removed, forcing the individual into the open, where he had to engage in work or fail.

I did the same with my problem employee, taking down her separation wall and expanding the whole front office into her space, which included reorganizing the filing system layout to provide added space and room to maneuver. It also allowed me to modify work assignments for all administrative staff, including moving her to the front window to handle customer contacts while still doing her budget work. The surprising outcome for her was that she blossomed, now being with the other office staff and no longer isolated. The whole office coordination improved dramatically, and I did it without the Board's approval, which only saw the success of how well everyone was getting along.

Also, with the change in township leadership, the new Mayor chose to pursue selling the municipal utility authority to a third-party private sector utility in order to receive an incentive payment of several million dollars, which the Township could use for their own needs, thereby terminating our independence — which the Mayor had little control over. I chose to fight this initiative by launching a speaker's bureau where I attended all local community meetings and spoke about the potential problems of a sale to a private party. The primary point was that rates would definitely go up because incentive payments needed to be reimbursed, profit margins had to be attained (generally 5%), reserves would be raided and possibly shifted to other communities that the private company served, and there would be little control by local entities. The message was clear, and the Mayor pulled the initiative after public sentiment turned against the sale. This only gave the Mayor more incentive to appoint utility board members who would vote me out as Executive Director.

At the same time, the Board decided to support my initiative to incentivize the employees, and I put forward a gain-sharing strategy that allowed the employees to receive an annual bonus based on the excess savings above and beyond the average savings of the last five years. So, if the average was 5%, and in the past year we achieved 7%, the difference saved (2%) was divided equally between all utility employees, including management. The adoption of this incentive proved effective in deterring efforts by union labor groups to make inroads into the Utility Operations personnel. It also served to demonstrate that management continued to support the employees, who never complained about the lack of critical equipment to meet daily work demands with the latest technical materials. I also finalized an operational audit of the Utility, which provided a clear direction for future spending and policy modification that offered profitable and sustainable changes benefiting both the ratepayers and the organization.

When I left the executive director role, I achieved my stated personal goal of leaving the utility better than I had found it. When I started, the infrastructure was old, the rate structure was out of sync with needs, a new wastewater plant was just being completed, corrective maintenance (CM) versus preventive maintenance (PM) was 65% over 35%, no reserves existed except for long-term debt, and water meter readings were done on a door-to-door manual-read basis. By the time I left, the bulk of the infrastructure was new, with no new debt due to impact fee payments. A new water plant was operating along with a new water tower, all the wastewater pumping stations had been renovated, water meters were new and being touch-read, reserves for maintenance totaled $8 million, capital funding reserves totaled $12 million, water and wastewater rates were lower than when I started (even after I had doubled them to meet expenditure demands), CM versus PM was 4% over 96%, and the Utility was scheduled to be out of debt in nine years.

The Board's attorney wrote me a letter of reference, defining my capabilities as rare and considering me one of only five exceptional CEOs in the entire state.

Lessons Learned From Utility and Local Government:

Driving changes when the changes are obvious should be your goal if you are the appointed leader. Never apologize, and be sure to tell the appointed body that you are there to raise the effectiveness of local services for the benefit of the public at large. Pushing a progressive agenda that gives your staff the tools to do their jobs more efficiently and removes the confusion of past leadership who waited to be told to evaluate or study a Board proposal. It also gives you a real opportunity to revise budgeted dollars on the fly so long as your argument for the new direction demonstrates a cost-benefit and doesn't increase authorized expenditures, time savings to fund planned outcomes, raises the bar on organizational and cultural interests, and can be used to advertise for new blood with higher standards of expectation because programs are being reported through a variety of sources as a great place to work. In many ways, it's the small things that help carry the message of progress. These may include:

1) Washing work trucks each day demonstrates a real interest in sustaining expensive equipment,

2) Having a set of standardized responses for field personnel so they can answer questions from the public up to a certain point and refer additional questions to the appropriate person,

3) Advertising well in advance plans for field work that may affect traffic patterns and service delivery, and

4) Participating in a speaker's bureau where senior leadership attends public events to discuss current and future plans well before a possible rate or tax increase comes into play so that budget impacts can be discussed and justified which helps to prepare the ground for potential cost adjustments affecting the public.

Trust in government is a task that must be encouraged, massaged, and delivered on every day of any year. Losing faith in government can happen based on one event that is badly handled. These may include the failure to prepare beforehand, which has not been pushed by management, and not having access to the right civic, business, and social resources to manage developing concerns, which may demonstrate the poor leadership qualities of managers who are led by political interests rather than driven by professional and higher moral and ethical standards of conduct.

It is also critical to have a progressive Board or Council that will give you the reins for implementing change without their intrusion so long as you have the message, justification, examples, and vision that gives them confidence that the budgeted changes are realistic and vital to on-going future plans, strategic and master plans. Also, in the face of mounting political pressure, never apologize or back down from what you see as the correct agenda for the organization you manage. You may lose your appointment, but you most likely will be found desirable by another entity that respects the professionalism and integrity of the office of Township Manager and Executive Director.

Despite being in a deteriorating relationship with newly appointed Board members who were following the direction of the Mayor to replace me, I found the experience to be highly satisfying to my professional confidence and understanding of my innate value to succeed despite the intrusion of politically motivated and self-serving demigods that are more interested in seizing power than driving growth and change for the better service to the community.

Ultimately, my progressive style and professional work ethic prevailed in building my value for future private sector opportunities. Building a personal brand that is attractive to other opportunities should be part of your personal goal, which is to rise through the ranks in any profession you may choose.

MID-ATLANTIC STATE ON THE EAST COAST

Agency Description:

The Governor came into office with plans to clean up a variety of outstanding issues. The Division within the Treasury Department was created to focus on three areas: schools, local government, and utilities (water/sewer/solid waste). Staff were drawn from experienced professionals who had operated in the targeted service areas, and they knew what they needed to look at to assess efficiency, program delivery, policy guidelines, and administrative responsibility. Schools and local governmentsare heavily reliant on local taxes to meet budget obligations.. The Treasury division needed to perform research and analysis of spending patterns and prepare a definition of opportunities to revise spending, which could include the consolidation of school districts and municipal entities. Utilities, being independent of direct local control other than the appointment of board members, required oversight to ensure activities reflected national associations' recommended procedures.

With the threat of firing due to revenge tactics by the new local Mayor, I was given a lifeline from the Governor's Office of the State to join a sub-division of the Department of the Treasury as a local government and Utility Specialist to help with two major fiscal initiatives:

(i) The Federal Appellate Court decision declared the State's Solid Waste Management Plan unconstitutional due to its restriction of interstate commerce, which put $1.5 billion of multi-county solid waste debt into jeopardy since the County Solid Waste Authorities could no longer include the debt obligation in their rate base pending corrective action.

(ii) Assist with the voluntary assessment of local governments wanting advice on how to reduce their reliance on property taxes with the introduction of potentially new efficiency measures.

Within four months of starting, I was promoted to Deputy Director of the Division with the departure of the former Director. This was not due to a poor management problem but a desire for the Director to move to a new opportunity. She had demonstrated the value of the Governor's program that had been created to address serious state agency problems impacting state agencies with track records of serious ethical, operational, fiscal, and contractual problems implementing stated policies and procedures adopted by the State Legislature and Governor's office. A new director was appointed several months later to take control, and he provided the two deputy directors with free reign to carry out our own plans so long as he was kept fully informed. The new director was transitioning out of state service and saw his role as more of a point of contact for the office. He monitored our actions to ensure no developments of concern could be allowed to undermine the office of the Governor.

I was directed by the State Treasurer to lead both initiatives in tandem, providing the opening presentation to City and Township Councils about the work my teams would be doing within all aspects of the organization, and I was to be the lead Specialist on the County Solid Waste Authority debt problem to assess their financial condition to determine suitable State financial assistance to these authorities to meet and service their debt obligations related to the construction of their transfer stations. The outcome of both tasks was this:

For item 1, the team found significant problems across all twenty-two county solid waste authorities, to the shock and dismay of the Governor's State Agency Heads and State Attorney General, who we reported to weekly in the Governor's conference room. Through the infield work, the detailed review of contracts and financial documents, interviews of key players, and testing of the accuracy of decisions made against the adopted policy, we determined that a regular maneuvering strategy was being implemented to blind their boards to real conditions on the ground. There were also numerous examples of political collusion involving board members,

professional consultants, and state legislators that were inappropri-
ate and allowed unfair fee structures to the benefit of certain legislative interests.

For example, in one instance, the attorney to a County Authority
had allowed negotiators to include language that allowed a major
electrical generating provider that used select solid waste materials
to power their steam generating systems to have access "in perpetu-
ity" to excess solid waste deliveries without remuneration that exceeded the targeted upper limit they paid for in raw materials. The
excess quantities were substantial and represented huge savings for
the private power generator. The attorney, who was also a state legislator, was given a sizeable contribution to his reelection campaign
each year in exchange for this perpetual understanding. In addition,
the contracted accountant to the Authority provided annual audit
documentation that was short on expenditure tables normally used
to define the balance sheet detailed justification. This, it can be assumed, allowed the agreement with the power company to go unno-
ticed for several years. Reporting this to the Governor's Committee
overseeing our work was not taken well and seriously caused real
consternation among them, knowing the players involved.

A second example of a county solid waste operation found a variety of unusual business practices. Specifically:

1. The agency assigned two drivers, who sat at the front doors of the administrative office waiting to deliver mail to board members and local council members in the county which paid $75,000 each.

2. The closure plan for the land fill had been over funded by $15 million yet it was still built into their rate base. The annual audit did not highlight this financial condition in any way.

3. The agency had $80 million in reserves that were undesignated nor committed to a particular purpose.

4. The agency had 150 excess employees associated with solid waste and funded from the rate base.

They essentially did not qualify for state financial support since they had substantial reserves and savings opportunities. Yet they demanded $10 million to address their debt concerns. I never learned what was agreed to after I had left the division.

When it was all over, the Commissioner of the State's Department of Environmental Protection, who had direct oversight of the solid waste program and was involved with the Governor's Committee, called me personally at my office. Since he couldn't afford to put his comments in writing to admit and apologize that his agency had been so totally unaware of the findings we submitted, he stated that he was seriously troubled by what we found. He appreciated my team's professionalism to mine the various authorities to learn what we did. Ultimately, the bond debt problem was determined to be about $300 million due to excessive reserves that were accessible to buy down the debt from the various solid waste authorities. Numerous recommendations were made to correct the reporting problems, and new checks and reporting measures were added to inspection guidelines to avoid future attempts to obscure financial irregularities.

Regarding item 2, the local governments were reluctant to request voluntary operational and fiscal audits. We did far fewer of these than the Governor had hoped for just because of their reluctance to give away historical precedents and their autonomy. This is despite the opportunity to correct some significant and some not-so-significant concerns that a little coordination could easily correct if they were to choose consolidation or county-wide service delivery over local delivery. Even though our findings were understated but glaringly beneficial, they were reluctant to proceed with most recommendations because they did not want to consider consolidation with a neighboring community to benefit from employing the philosophy of using an economy of scale. Plus, they didn't want to admit the level of inefficiency they had, and a commitment to our recommendations would weaken their control and power over their planned destinies. The public benefit was their last issue of concern. The topic of consolidation was found to be extremely controversial despite the obvious benefits since, in most people's minds, the demarcation of budget responsibility for shared and/or consolidated services was never defined well enough to gain their support. Presentations of our findings and recommendations were always made during a closed session of the Council. In the end, no one chose to proceed. Consider yes, implement no.

Lessons learned from State Government employment:

For the second time, I was promoted to lead a significant division of state government within the Department of Treasury from my junior Project Management role. I had been initially hired to serve as a specialist who understood local government, independent utilities, and municipal authorities within the State. It was clear that my team had a voice in my appointment to the Deputy role, and I chose to maintain a flat organizational structure such that I made the decisions on work activity and final report outline, but the work activity was driven by the team based on deliverables and progress reports which I used to report weekly to the Governor's Committee overseeing our work. I found that my prior work history in State government from a mid-west state was useful for report preparation and public presentation of progress reports. The findings we identified were used to target work assignments and drove the packaging of report documents. I also found that my independent nature to challenge normal political interests rather than subdue my reporting to less onerous comments served to demonstrate the seriousness of our findings and highlight the failure of various state agencies to monitor successfully the activities of target entities. The prior work I had done in local government from a mid-west state provided me with the wherewithal to delve into specific documents and source data, which I trained the team to use for their own work. As a result, our findings were in many ways explosive and astounding to agency heads unused to being undermined by a small team of specialists that found more problems than their own sizeable enforcement staff who had years of exposure to their activities.

Despite the clarity of our findings and specific lists of recommendations to correct problems, many of the recommendations were never imposed, and little was done to maneuver specific political interests into amending their activities.

Later, I learned that efforts to find me in order to influence my governmental opportunities were made by several political leaders in the State due to the damage our reporting had done to them.

However, their efforts were stymied due to my taking a position in the private sector, whose head office was in another state.

Joining The Private Sector Put Me Into A Whole New Lane Of Sleuthing

Private Company Description: The internationally recognized environmental engineering firm I worked for provides a broad range of services that involve marketing, promotion, proposal generation, design support, project management, subject matter expertise, interim management support, software implementation, and connectivity, engineering and construction management, and so on for water, sewer, power, transportation, buildings, dams, and so many other specializations. I was assigned to the management consulting division.

Assignment: SMALL COMMUNITY WITHIN MID-ATLANTIC STATE

My last duty, performing a voluntary audit for the State Treasury division, led to a local government and its semi-independent Water Commission that demonstrated significant illegitimate activities the new Mayor knew would require new leadership of the latter entity. The criticality of the leadership situation was sizeable to the point that without a strong manager running the utility, the community could have been faced with a major lawsuit, tax implications, and a state takeover of the entire community. The private engineering firm the mayor selected to administer the transition to the new leadership team knew me based on prior work at my old Municipal Utility, where we used them for our contractual engineering requirements. Since the firm knew me and the mayor liked how I introduced the State-sponsored organizational audit and my team, I was hired by the consulting firm to take on the Manager's role of the Water Commission, effectively leaving my state position.

I was challenged immediately by the State's ethics commission for potentially not stepping down or informing my immediate director that I was in negotiations with the private contractor who was working in conjunction with the local organization I was evaluating. The conflict of interest was palpable, but I was able to demonstrate that I had removed myself immediately from on-site involvement in the project, distributing assignments to each involved state agent I was running and having them report directly to the Director. Ultimately, the state agreed with me, and the red flag over my new appointment was removed by my new firm.

The role that I chose to accept as my first project assignment turned out to be what my new Consulting firm determined after the job was finished, one and a half years later, as the most difficult and challenged client they had ever served. My role as Interim General Manager had my firm report to me as the client, which was a bit disconcerting since I had just been hired by them. The prior contract manager (CM) of the Water Commission had previously been an employee of the Commission. However, through collusion with the Board of Directors, he created a private contracting company and took on the role of Contract Manager. He immediately hired all the former division heads to be contractors under his personal business office with higher salaries. Their allegiance and loyalty were to him until I forced them to reestablish an employment contract with the Commission at no loss for wages. Five lawsuits were attempted by the CM to disengage my firm and reestablish their contract. All were defeated. The City Council and elected State legislators were privately in the CM's orbit based on regular political contributions from the companies he ran, benefitting from his control of the Water Commission. The mayor, however, was independent and stood for good government. The prior CM had worked with a member of the City's Finance staff to steal the financial management software shared with the City that the deceased Finance Director (former IBM staffer) had designed and provided for the City. They took advantage of the software being run on Water Commission computers that were not housed on City property. His death allowed the CM and his Finance partner to take ownership without notice by the city, where the Commission ended up paying an annual fee for the use of software they already owned. In addition, to expand their profit potential, the CM procured a Beta version of an early Geographic Information System (GIS) mapping database, which he used to promote and establish contractual inter-local service agreements with four surrounding communities. The Commission would provide both water distribution and wastewater collection services. However, our review of the inter-local service agreements drafted by the former CM turned out to be money-losing contracts requiring the Commission to cover many of those community's operational service costs. In addition, the CM failed to follow the contract language requiring quarterly updates of service activity. The Comptroller of the Commission also turned out to be an independent contract employee to the former CM and regularly used subterfuge to provide updates, financial information, and private board discussion information to the former CM.

From the first day, the consulting team was swimming against a fire hose of problems. On day one, my consulting firm was fired by the Board, and the Mayor vetoed that action. On day two, the firm that had stolen the finance software said they would terminate the City's and Water Commission's use of the software within three months. Hence, I needed to fund the replacement of the Finance software. On day three, one of the communities we contracted to support suffered a major rain event that overwhelmed a control valve and allowed biological material to be flushed into their water system from an area supply lake. This initiated an immediate boil water notice until flushing and testing cleared the problem. I was on the local area metropolitan TV news that evening describing our plan to address and act on correcting the problem. On day four, we received the first of five lawsuits from the former CM to reverse the decision and allegations made about him.

At the initial presentation before the City Council, they attempted to destabilize the utility by rejecting my request to amend the Capital Project Bond Ordinance to take advantage of savings from earlier projects to be used for the replacement of the corrupted finance software with a Windows-based system. I told the City

Council, with 300 members of the public sitting behind me, that I would, therefore, use all available cash to proceed without them, which we did. They then chose to act on an attempt to create a Municipal Utility Authority where they would appoint themselves to the Board and give themselves significant salaries, with the source of the application coming from the Comptroller who was under their influence even though he was being paid by the Water Commission. At the same time, the former CM who owned half of a firm that performed the pipeline maintenance and repair services throughout all five communities, slowed responsiveness down where the Commission had inter-local service agreements. This same pipeline entity attempted to cash strap the Commission by quietly opening water hydrants in the lower part of the City such that the Commission needed to procure a backup water supply from a private water company to meet daily demand until the leak was found a day later. The intent being to demonstrate the poor management capabilities of myself and my consulting firm. Finally, the area around the Commission's head office was regularly subject to gangland gun fights and thefts of water repair equipment from work trucks, which had many of us feeling a bit unsettled.

We immediately brought in specialists to reverse engineer the third party's password access to the finance software and a GIS Beta system that was also controlled off-sight. The service connection was terminated to retake ownership and control, which ended annual payments to that firm. This was justified by the fact that the contractor had stolen the software several years prior, and the former Contract Manager had agreed to pay him for his services and to generate payments to himself as co-owner of the IT firm.

The next effort was to get more control of payment obligations from customers who were delinquent by as much as one month to three years. The Commission had no policy to terminate service to delinquent customers. I immediately advertised and gave a thirty-day grace period to catch up. I also arranged to meet with all four Community City Managers to renegotiate the inter-local service agreements and to redefine the expectations they were assuming we provided. I proceeded to do a full review of the operations facilities to get a sense of the condition of critical assets. I also asked my firm to immediately initiate the preparation of a strategic plan that I would provide intel from my operational audit of both capital needs and operations shortcomings. It was interesting to find the well field for the Commission was in a granite rock aquifer where the pumping units had not been shut down for repair in more than forty years. Essentially, the Commission was facing a potential major failure of water service if they were ever to go down with no backup pumps and motors in inventory.

We proceeded with a plan to replace the Finance software and rolled it out over six months, running parallel systems for one month. This effort included attempts by office staff to browbeat and abuse trainers on the software to the point that I had to threaten immediate dismissal of any example of this problem. Throughout, meetings were being held privately, without my involvement, to package an application to become a Municipal Utility Authority between members of the City Council, the Commission Board, and the Comptroller. I finally learned of the meetings when they were in an advanced stage and ready to submit to the State Finance Board, which authorized such requests. When the application came up for consideration, I attended the meeting and spoke with the Executive Director of the Finance Board informing him that this should not pass for any reason due to the true nature and goal of the parties involved. Luckily, he knew me and trusted me due to my earlier work with the Treasury Department. The application failed, and within several months, a permanent Manager was hired, allowing me to move on to a new assignment. We had also been under immediate observation by the State regarding the management concerns we and the city had been suffering from by the lawsuits and actions of the City Council. I left knowing that the situation was well in hand.

Lessons Learned From Interim Management and Reorganization: Even though I represented a target of scorn by the former CM and a majority of the City Council, having access to a large, talented consulting firm to offer ideas and change management opportunities was critical to correcting the work culture and move the organization in a new direction. My leadership strategy offered a chance to coordinate the labor pool even though there was a battle happening between differing masters, myself, and the former CM, who still had access to his former team of leaders. Understanding these organizational challenges, I decided at the outset to establish my office in the Board room since I could see everything going on in the building, who came in, and who was talking to who. My Firm did not agree with me about not taking the Manager's Office, but the threat I offered and visual control served to correct many problems they couldn't realize.

I pushed a vision of public service, quality service, professionalism, and positive engagement in front of the public to build up the value of the staff's presence and purpose during several City Council meetings that were regularly attended on average by about 300 members of the public. I argued that leadership must always be open and clear about the mission and value of the utility to the community's quality of life. Reporting on the changes being introduced through retrenchment from contract management to centralized control served as a major cost justifier to manage budgeted expenses. Introducing technology, new training requirements, enhancing the tracking of data metrics, and direct communication by a progressive leader were central to changing organizational behavior. This approach offered both a new work culture and budget-driven improvements that they were just beginning to realize. I also argued that being able to demonstrate service enhancements while maintaining a status quo budget using new efficiency measures would be a game changer that could improve public sentiment dramatically. In the end, chances for work culture improvements with the introduction of new training and cross-training opportunities served to be invaluable for raising the bar of staff satisfaction.

The situation I left behind was a difficult animal to get under control. There was a level of corruption that had been terminated with my additional reporting requirements and the replacement of the financial team with new professionals approved by the State office monitoring the Commission. But the influence moved off-site, and I expect it would still play a subtle role in the Commission's future.

Assignment: MAJOR CITY ON THE GREAT LAKES

I moved on to assist with a management audit of a large regional water utility on Lake Michigan that had been operating essentially the same way as it had since the early 1900s. The real fact of the matter was this utility was not that unusual from others like it and of the same size across the US. It had a large, unionized workforce under the control of the city, where the Mayor assigned the Commissioner. It was clear that historically, the appointment of a commissioner was determined by blind loyalty to the Mayor's Office who expected union labor was part of the Mayor's domain when he needed them. It was also understood that consideration of new efficiencies should not include downsizing staff positions that were needed for various political activities that occurred throughout the year, every year.

True to form, the Commissioner demonstrated no interest in the Utility and was only biding his time until reappointment to another position within City government. When we finished our two-year-long assessment, and we told him that we had found $30 million in savings opportunities out of a $200 million budget, he wasn't impressed. We also reported that they could downsize their operations staff by 350 out of 2,000 or so employee positions, taking advantage of planned retirements and normal staff attrition for other opportunities. He asked how long it would take, and we responded in three or four years because of retraining, new software application implementations, creating new job titles and work descriptions, instituting new procedures with treatment systems to incorporate SCADA (Supervisory Control and Data Acquisition), and implementing a new water meter reading initiative and billing system. He said that was too long and he wouldn't agree to proceed. This was troubling because of our findings.

1) The existing water meter reading methodology was antiquated and dangerous. Essentially, the meter reading staff maintained a vault at each of their staging sites that contained keys to every property receiving City water. Essentially, they could enter and take readings from meters located in the basements of most properties, residential and commercial. The insurance implications for possible theft were enormous. The performance metric was 80 reads per day per meter reader which was extremely inefficient with a high labor cost.

2) In addition, half of the metropolitan area had water meters, and the other half did not. The latter were charged a flat rate based on the number of faucets. This meant that if you had a pool, you got free water since it wasn't measured when you filled it.

3) The maintenance staff relied on a Rolodex where each page listed work requirements. There were twelve months of segmented work schedules where, for every day of every month duty assignments listed work for the day. Staff carried out the work, no matter if it was needed or not, only required an hour of time, and the rest of the day was free even if repair parts were available or not, and there was no centralized list of parts available in inventory in the various storage areas that were housed between multiple sites.

4) The City's water system was pressurized using pumping stations and did not have water towers to balance system pressures because they would scar the visual horizon. This expensive approach was further found to have serious maintenance and replacement implications when it was learned that the custom-built and very large pumping units that were housed in city block-sized buildings were more than 75 to 100 years old and had received very little maintenance. None of the pump stations were built by the same manufacturer. Spare parts did not exist since the original manufacturers had gone out of business, which required custom parts to be manufactured. In addition, each pump station had interconnection valve portals that maintained separate water pressure districts throughout the metropolitan area. The intent was to use the portals to maintain water pressure in multiple districts when a district pump station was

down for maintenance. However, these large interconnects had never been used in all those years.

5) Safety supplies for field personnel performing repairs, traffic control, and so on were procured for the employees on a centralized basis. Yet the manager of that safety sub-division never distributed the safety supplies. The field teams had to get them through other means, but the fact of this negligence was a significant complaint from union employees.

6) There was only one site to clock in for work even though there were multiple staging sites for work initiation that were separated by at least an hour of commute. This alone was seriously expensive and reduced available work hours dramatically, impacting many workers.

7) We also found that the City Finance Office was manipulating the use of Water Funds with the City's General Fund because the monthly water bills guaranteed constant cash flow, whereas the City was reliant on tax payments and other fees that were inconsistent with the timing of their payment demands. Utility revenue is not considered general tax revenue, even though that is how it was treated. Lost interest earnings affected income expectations and challenged adequate collateral necessary to cover contract obligations.

8) We suspected that the Water Utility was covering the cost of worker's compensation payments for both the Utility and the City. The fees being paid annually were over $5 million, yet the utility only had five individuals on average out for medical leave in any one year out of a pool of more than 2,000 employees.

9) We found that a contract with a gaseous chlorine supplier had never been finalized for more than nine years. The contractor continued to send a pressurized train car weekly to the water treatment facilities that went through the center of the City. This meant the company was assuming the goodwill of the City that they would ultimately pay. However, the insurance liability of this relationship was stunning because the City might have been held liable if an event were to occur.

10) We found the solution for controlling ice buildup during winter months at the access point for water from Lake Michigan was to use small pieces of dynamite thrown into the center of the water access structure. The pressure wave shook loose ice buildup. The method was effective but exceedingly dangerous to carry out.

11) Finally, the unions were fully behind the recommendations, yet the Commissioner couldn't be bothered to entertain the report recommendations.

It took five years after we completed the report for a commissioner to be appointed who took our report and implemented everything. He came from within the ranks of the Water Utility, an engineer who had always endorsed the recommendations for change outlined in our report. The corporate culture changed dramatically under his control to the benefit of the metropolitan community. The surprising aspect of our findings was that senior management historically knew of the problems but were never curious nor incentivized to drive amendments to their corporate structure. Progress through normal development within the environmental industry was never realized nor desired. I would surmise that this is how Flynt Michigan's water crisis was allowed to occur.

The recommendations implemented generally included:

1) Introduction of SCADA (Supervisory Control and Data Acquisition) for two of the largest water treatment facilities in the United States, which contributed to the staff reduction opportunity for data tracking, remote systems control, monitoring security (access and televised), and the ability to adjust chemical additions on the fly.

2) Plans were implemented to hire a custom contractor who built large water pumping systems to initiate the replacement of

each pumping unit to standardize around one company design for parts and supply management for long-term repairs.

3) Implementation of a work management system to monitor repair and maintenance planning and to improve the scheduling of preventive maintenance activities and the tracking of available parts held in inventory.

4) Implementation of a standardized timecard system used by all City offices such that employees could sign in at their staging sites for field assignments and eliminate wasted commuting hours to a central office location, which avoided potential overtime charges.

5) Implementation of a plan I prepared for an automated meter reading system that integrated with the water customer billing system and had the water utility coordinate with the metropolitan gas company to perform drive-by reads of properties for both utilities. This eliminated the need to retain the keys to all the residential and commercial properties. This allowed the utility to shift staff from meter reading to field repair activities and planned retirements.

6) The Utility carried out downsizing job titles from over 300 to less than 100 and established improved guidelines for structuring development within those job titles.

7) All customer billing properties were standardized to receive a water meter eligible for automated meter reading to improve accuracy based on actual water consumption.

8) Safety training was linked to the independent wastewater treatment utility that carried out one of the best examples of safety training for most environmental entities in the state.

Lessons Learned From Management and Operational Analysis of a Large Organization:

Real leadership, dedicated and professional leadership, and engaged and focused leadership is the agent that encourages a team spirit, regardless of a union versus non-union situation. This provides an atmosphere to develop a work environment, driving progress, that is sustainable and principled. The failure of leadership to change a century of historical work patterns that were knowingly poor work practices but following the old adage, "if it ain't broke, don't fix it," is a very destructive program to follow. This is a pattern demonstrated by many local government and utility organizations across the country because what is known is comfortable, and weaknesses can be explained away. Change has to be managed, and new procedural guidelines have to be prepared along with new reporting requirements. This kind of change is hard for many to take on. But to be fair, strong managers with a vision that can be embraced by senior staff can make significant improvements that allow real improvements that eliminate old frustrations and procedural hurdles. It can also embolden reluctant leaders to develop stretch goals that push their risk envelop, which can build their confidence and character.

Assignment: MID-WEST CITY IN THE PLAINS STATES

As I stated earlier, operating conditions and organizational structural problems at utilities were not unique to large or smaller entities. The next project I led was the first asset management project my firm had ever done. It was for a city whose wastewater utility had been turned over to a third-party contract firm with the intended result being one of efficient return on a 10-year investment but failed miserably in practice. It was obvious at the outset that prior city administrations had failed miserably to package viable contract language that would enforce real oversight and control because there should have been a regular on-site review and reporting requirement for the old contract firm, which wasn't the case. What we found was tantamount to deliberate negligence where the city had no recourse to bring charges based on the lack of clarity in the contract language.

Therefore, the project we were to perform was to create a new baseline which added oversight responsibilities for the city to meet. Issuing the next new contract for a third-party contract operation for the wastewater utility would be dramatically different. The intent was to:

1) Build a capital budget to put the facility back in full original design condition,

2) Provide a maintenance schedule to maintain and sustain the facility and

3) Establish a cost basis of the facility that the new contract operator would be required to meet and/or exceed at the point of contract termination or renewal in twenty years.

What we started with was challenging. Not only did the prior contract firm walk away with the database from their computerized maintenance management system such that we had no historical information, but they also left a facility broken and misused, which required significant investment to rehabilitate the facilities to their original standard operating condition. I set the project budget amount and the expected time commitments to carry out a full criticality and condition assessment of all key assets and the creation of a new preventive maintenance scheduling database for those same assets. A separate group prepared the cost estimate for the rehabilitation of the facility. As we walked through following the flow of wastewater treatment, we found the headworks crumbling and filled to the brim with grease and gravel such that the traveling trash screen was buried in debris and out of service. This forced waste flow to pass through the headworks to the primaries, where the traveling skim units had been sheared off due to blocks of grease, the size of golf carts, in the bottom of the tank. The primary served as the headwork in this instance, allowing secondary treatment to be without hindrance, but most moving parts out of service time and needing maintenance. Over the course of three months, we completed our work, meeting the required schedule to the satisfaction of the client.

As project leader, I advised the City Finance Director, Budget Officer, and Public Works Manager that their ignorance of the operating philosophy of the former contract operator was their responsibility and that they were negligent in their lack of oversight. I recommended that the next contract should include language for monthly oversight, meetings, and scheduled/unscheduled walk-throughs to assure them that this major capital investment they were having to make would not be repeated. A clear definition of preventive maintenance scheduling would be followed with their office retaining an original copy of the preferred schedule in order to prevent the selected contractor from revising the preventive maintenance schedule without a full open discussion and justification with the city. They had to avoid the problem of contractors delaying maintenance, which is the contractor's cost problem to the point where replacement or rehabilitation must be done when it becomes a city capital expense. This saves the contractor's budget and improves their profit margin at the expense of the city. I found out that there was a similar example of this delaying strategy operating at a large Midwest City that was shared by the Executive Director of that community at the time.

Lessons Learned From a Mid-sized Community Sewer Organization:

Like the prior large organization, leadership and oversight are everything. Ignoring the obvious when you contract for services with a third party without defining service expectations or ongoing reportable service metrics and defined deliverables to be done prior to contract termination is a real failure in management that should have consequences. This is due to the cost of cleaning up and repairing the problems that led the city to experience serious cost exposure. Private sector operators are valuable if the right language and defined expectations are clearly outlined to establish a viable business model and oversight relationship. These same interests, however, are never your friend if their unstated modus operandi is to extract maximum profit out of a short-sighted contract description.

Assignment: MAJOR UTILITY ON THE EAST COAST

From the mid-west, I moved on to take on one of the biggest utility operations in the United States. Again, as stated with the first two large and small utilities, the failure of management to maintain their facilities and operating conditions was missing spectacularly overall. The project was to perform a comprehensive assessment of all metropolitan facilities operating under the control of Water Supply (dams, reservoirs, pipelines, siphons, large watershed capture zone, roads, numerous wastewater facilities impacting the water reservoirs), Wastewater Treatment (14 secondary wastewater treatment facilities averaging 300 mgd and eight associated dewatering facilities) and Water and Sewer Operations (numerous water pumping stations, extensive number of sewer pumping stations, force mains, distribution mains, and sewer system pipelines). Overseeing the repair and capital activities of these divisions included an Engineering Design and Construction (EDC) group.

It was again obvious that the problem for the failure to maintain, rehabilitate, replace, and renew critical assets in a densely populated city with over 200 years of history and leading-edge design and implementation projects for its day more than a century in the past was management. The growth aspects and size of the service needs were understood and known. Yet, the city ignored the problems of maintenance as many governments do by reducing maintenance budgets to avoid raising taxes or utility rates when there is this unconscionable belief that "Oh, we can get a few more years out of the infrastructure before we need to do anything." As many cities and utilities have found, that argument fails miserably when the systems fail and the price doubles from original estimates because now it's an emergency when before it was normal maintenance that could be scheduled. Yet, they always seem to miss the obvious. When senior managers are appointed who are followers rather than leaders driven by strategic thinking, budget efficiency, system performance, and crisis avoidance using forward thinking and planning to handle growth concerns, there will always be a failure of critical systems. This leads to Councils and Boards assigning blame to senior leadership to avoid their involvement in the decision that led to the failure. This was clearly what we found at this location.

The Commissioner of the environmental department, at the outset, was a former planner, and when he took on the position, his personal assessment was that the Department was seriously behind in its repair and rehabilitation spending. In reality, my team determined that the city had built a Rolls Royce of facilities that were of very high quality and exemplified architectural design gems involving a distinguished landscape architect, clearly from an earlier time, between 75 and 140 years ago. The goal of the project was to establish a criticality value and a likelihood of failure value that followed the guidelines of a US Airforce assessment model and generated an Asset Risk Index (ARI) number using a ten-point scale for both measures. The resulting ARI value determined a degree of risk prioritized on a scale from 1 to 100. The intent was to allow the generated ARI values to prioritize capital repairs and replacement expenditures over a ten-year capital program schedule.

What we found early was the mistake EDC had made, allowing a large number of professional engineering firms to be assigned to dedicated wastewater facilities to determine what capital projects needed to be done. Each firm would then prepare the engineering design and perform the contract management work for all those projects. This essentially put the wolf in charge of which sheep they would feast on based on a 10-year $17 billion capital program. We also learned that wastewater treatment facility managers regularly deferred cash-based maintenance activities to save money in their annual budget even though the repairs could have been completed on average within six months. Instead, they chose to shift repair responsibility to EDC to be scheduled for capital funding (long-term debt) that averaged 3-4 years to fund and carry out. This represented a major efficiency breakdown and a cost contributor by delaying work for several years.

I earned a little respect from senior leadership in the Mayor's Office of Management and Budget (OMB) and the Utility Department during a meeting to discuss the next steps at the outset of the project. I asked a question in response to a comment from a division head about why they needed our ARI data to move forward. My question was simple: "How much had the City invested in the past 20 or more years to maintain and rehabilitate their facilities?" The response was the Department ran a $17 billion dollar 10-year capital program which clearly had more delayed projects than project implementations. I stated that your statements mean nothing to me. I asked to see the latest bond prospectus issued by the Department through OMB and the City Finance Board. I then said turn to the balance sheet and look at the number on the bottom. That number defined the value of their on-going capital investment after depreciation and new capital investment were included. The Finance Officer looked and said, "This can't be right. It says only $16 million dollars." This was a stunning statement because, in reality, this represented the value of more than $250 billion of assets under their control.

Our on-site review over the course of three years validated this financial reality and found significant condition challenges everywhere. For example, one consulting firm had asked for $1 billion worth of rehabilitation at one waste treatment facility. Another asked for $800 million for theirs, and another was undergoing a $1.5 billion upgrade. At a second meeting, the head of Water Supply asked the head of EDC how the ARI project would help justify the funding they had and any new funding they may need to correct their extensive problems. I offered to answer that question since the head of EDC didn't have an answer that I knew of. Basically, I stated that the Department annually submitted an extensive list of projects about two feet high on green bar computer paper to OMB. OMB had no means to validate if the funding request was accurate, strategically targeted, prioritized, or what. I stated that adding a three-color coded risk assessment model based on criticality and condition would demonstrate the priority assets needing immediate, runner, and future planned priorities within the 10-year planning horizon. Essentially, this would allow the Department that owned the risk to transfer ownership of that risk to OMB, who is responsible for authorizing funding since they now know the degree of risk exposure the city had. They also knew that OMB now owned the risk of failing to meet a comprehensive capital investment strategy. All present heard this and agreed that this project needed to move forward.

I divided my team into three focus groups for each Bureau and matched them with engineers, chief operators, chief mechanics and operators and sent them out to perform risk assessments. It started slowly since it was a learning process that the in-house engineering group would take over and perform annually in preparation for the next capital budget submittal. They were all suspicious of the outcome until they saw the results and came back to us with a request to revisit many of the assets they had scored because they were not necessarily honest in their review and preferred to correct the outcome to reflect the true priority and condition of the select assets.

During the rollout of this project, an incident occurred which highlighted the importance of completing this project. There was a City-wide power outage for several hours, which allowed the combined storm and sewer pipes to overwhelm valves and flush millions of gallons of contaminated water directly into the local river. The Federal EPA responded immediately by sending in a Federal Monitor to assess and lay blame on the problem. Three Wastewater Treatment Plant Managers were found negligent and spent time in jail for it. A major example of negligence was the failure to exercise black start generators that provided backup electrical power to ensure that startup power was available for larger natural gas-driven generators necessary to power up the treatment facilities when electrical power was lost. On our risk assessment tables, they were one of the top three priority items for maintenance and repair to the mayor's relief.

One wastewater treatment facility stood out. A 400 mgd secondary treatment facility that had been operating since the turn of the 20th century. My first on-site glimpse of the operating units was telling. For example, there were large gaps in the air flow feeding the secondary treatment channels that stirred the mixed liquor and fed oxygen to the organic biomass, treating the final effluent before solids removal and chlorination of effluent prior to release to the river. I wondered about this and asked the Chief Operator if it concerned him. He stated not really since they were meeting permits. Being suspicious and since we were assessing both the criticality of system assets and their condition, I told him he would need to empty at least four trains of the secondary units. He indicated that they had never done that before in all his time at the facility, and he had been there more than 25 years. I told him that is the very reason I'm asking him to do it. He said, come back in two days, and it will be done. Two days later, a major problem was identified that had been unknown for potentially 20 years or more. There were holes, the size of pickup trucks, in several places of both sets of units that served to separate the effluent materials. The aeration pipeline that carried oxygen under pressure to the bottom of the concrete walls on both sides of each channel had been rusted out and broken in several places. The Chief Operator was shaking his head, realizing just what this meant for the rest of the treatment trains, totaling about 16 tanks. The scoring told a serious problem existed for this facility and was repeated at all the other treatment facilities as well.

At wastewater treatment facilities, the number one priority for each was the reliability of the main sewage pumps that lifted waste flows entering the headworks up ten to twenty feet, which allowed untreated wastewater to use gravity to flow through the treatment process. The pumps were not regularly taken out of service to ensure they maintained maximum pumping capability, which required changing the impeller, which degraded over time. This caused pump efficiency to fall over time to less than 30 percent and could burn out the pump.

It wasn't unusual to find large transport pipelines on site that had been abandoned and a newer pipe installed next to it to carry the flow with no plans to remove the old pipe, which had been there for a good number of years. Site management was appalling.

An earlier example of a major cost-saving initiative was pursued back in the 1980s. The project was to reduce electrical service cost charges when power rates were very high at sewer pumping stations that required a low labor investment. The Department had decided to shift from large electric motor-driven sewer pumps with cutting blades needed to emulsify materials in the waste stream to smaller energy-efficient pump motors with no cutting blades. The Department learned quickly that the new pumps and motors were easily overwhelmed by waste materials and foreign objects (sheets, towels, wood chunks, blankets, and so on). The solution required a large staff investment to clean the wet wells and pumps almost daily due to the loss of cutting blades with these new motors. Essentially, the Department had implemented a low labor/high energy cost pumping situation to a high labor/lower energy cost environment which ultimately failed to realize the cost reduction target represented by high energy efficient motors. During our project review, my team encouraged EDC to install muffin monsters at the various pumping stations that would take over the duty of the cutting blades and lower the demand for labor. The real issue was that these latter units were available when the department transitioned yet, they failed to anticipate nor fund this critical piece that would ensure maintaining a lower labor cost requirement.

We also found another costly engineering mistake in the area of a large stormwater pumping station that had been built under a wide concrete plaza. Access to the station was through an in-ground vault with stairs that receded down to a subterranean level. This site had been a test case for the Department which wanted to manage the influence of high river conditions affecting normal storm flows to the river. The pump station had never been used for its original purpose to capture storm flows needing treatment. Instead, flows were captured and then discharged back to the adjacent River when the facility wasn't being surged due to high tide conditions. Originally, the flows were to be sent from the station to a nearby sewer pumping station and then on for treatment at a wastewater treatment facility. This never happened. There were three large circular catchment units that included motors to maintain materials in suspension. Oxygen was to be added to keep odors under control, but it had never been used. The overall design failure was due to the surface plaza cap. The engineers learned that the ceiling was too low to service the pumps and motors, and no ceiling trap doors had been installed to provide access for removal. We recommended decommissioning and removal from the overall inventory of assets.

At this stage, the focus shifted to the water pumping stations spread across the city to support the higher elevations where water pressure could fall off without the stations. The general condition of the water pumping stations was both old and outdated. The power coils being used were of another era. They were oversized, danger-ous to be exposed to, and very much relied upon to operate each day. The importance of these stations was to ensure water pressure for about 5% of the metropolitan area met a City guideline requiring a minimum of 40 psi up to the second floor of any business or resi-dence. The standard pressures (1,200 psi) within the supply tunnels serving the city and feeding the distribution mains were able to push water pressure to the fourth floor of most buildings. One station had old electric motors used to increase pressure upstream that were housed inside glass walls with a sign saying, "Do not enter when operating." The reason being the motors regularly arced blue rain-bows between the motors and the power control cabinets, which is extremely hazardous. This station dates back to the prior century and still it ran regularly. We knew of no plans to update the station, but we did perform the risk index assessment.

The large number of supply lakes serving the city required dam maintenance, siphon maintenance which delivered water between supply lakes, and land management for over 2,000 square miles. The Bureau ensured the smooth operation of seven wastewater treat-ment facilities that emptied into the supply lakes was reliable, and the road management network around the lakes was maintained. All were evaluated for risk and prioritized for repairs.

At the end of the project, I was able to submit a snapshot document that color-coded the sections of the major facilities based on the detailed list of risk assets on the supporting database to demonstrate the degree of risk the Department owned. This document easily justified additional funding of $9 billion for a new total of $26 billion over the 10-year Capital Program. The Federal Monitor found the document one of the best tools for decision-making he had ever seen, especially for such a large operation. The real value that came out of this project was that implementation allowed for the gradual change of engineering staff within EDC to become project managers. They now assign projects to engineering contractors rather than being told by these same consultants what those projects should be. The organizational culture improved dramatically, and their confidence in carrying out their duties was markedly boosted. I was also able to take the outcome of this project on the road to three national and international conferences as a significant example of how to manage the introduction of new modern operating procedures using the philosophy of asset management to correct significant mismanagement practices and policy oversights in a large organization serving a major international city.

Lessons Learned From a Large City Water and Wastewater Capital Prioritization Initiative:

Just like the earlier example of a large organization, when the light bulb went on after they learned just how badly they were performing maintenance and sustaining an engineering marvel when first built and essentially a train wreck today, they were astounded. They couldn't accept the fact that the whole operation was on life support and was declining quickly. This was one of the largest utility operations in the country, serving an international financial center of the world that had not been investing effectively in its infrastructure. The dramatic change by the professional engineering staff to become drivers of projects was in sharp contrast to their earlier practice of being a patient follower of third-party motivations, profiting from a weak management philosophy. It was a major win for the organization and the public at large. By prioritizing assets needing maintenance and/or replacement by tracking operating conditions and the effect of a strong preventive maintenance program, the Department has been able to turn around a failing business model in very short order. They accepted ownership of the past management problems and embraced organizational change, promoting regular and consistent monitoring and review of critical asset groups. Performance metrics have also been put in place to measure progress over time.

Assignment: LARGE CITY IN THE NORTH-EAST

The consolidation of water and wastewater departments represents an opportunity to take advantage of an economy of scale, share safety training, allow cross-support of vehicle repair and maintenance, share administrative interests, and allow cross-training to encourage the development of staff and their capacities to name a few. A large city in New England wanted to both consolidate utility divisions and assign a new joint division head from one of the two existing division managers.

We suspected that the orientation of the new joint initiative was one to consolidate control under one leader who would be accountable to the Director of the Department and to the City Manager ultimately. This turned out to be true in the worst possible way.

The evaluation of the two divisions was relatively straightforward. The Wastewater Division had a manager who never held a staff meeting, gave unlimited control of wastewater treatment over to the plant manager, and expected his operations team to function under their own initiative. He had a relationship with the Head of Engineering and Public Works, who oversaw the two divisions, and therefore, using that connection, his expectations were measured from a distance and unowned, yet he assumed and got control through his relationship, which everyone knew about. Staff morale was low because operations were basically unsupported by leadership.

The Water Division had a real leader who encouraged his staff to push the latest and best ideas in the water industry, shared decision-making by asking for their ideas on solutions to problems, and made sure they had the necessary tools to do their jobs. The report on consolidation provided recommendations to easily roll out the initiative, providing several tightening practices for wastewater, and we recommended the Water Chief for the Division Head role.

The Department Head selected the Wastewater Chief, and the Water Chief resigned immediately, knowing that he couldn't work for him. This is a clear example of the problem many organizations face when leadership chooses friends who are loyal and will follow their lead without understanding the damage this causes to the larger body of staff. Since the new Division Head was not a hands-on manager nor had the respect of his staff, the consolidation was in many ways damaged since he couldn't build a relationship with his team nor offer a clear vision of what needed to be done.

Lessons Learned From Water and Sewer Department Consolidation:

From the outset of any project, driving change that will have a major impact on operational coordination and working relationships should not presuppose that leadership's personal operational model they envisioned will survive. It is generally understood that the distinct and deliberate recommendations made by a third party with no motives other than maintaining a professional distance and providing a bird's eye view of operational realities will not affect a predetermined outcome. The deliberate ruin of a critical department within city government just to reward a weak personal friend over a clearly superior leader with real staff engagement is in many ways criminal in its intent and destructive in its outcome. This example must be avoided.

Assignment: WATER UTILITY NEAR THE NATIONS CAPITOL

The regional wastewater treatment and potable water reuse facility located West of the nation's capital is a critical element in the growth and development of bedroom community areas outside the city. As such, the treatment requirements are significant for assuring high-quality potable water is released to a 180-million-gallon reservoir used as a supply source serving the four neighboring communities. The project was to perform an operational and financial assessment of the utility, where I was to review the financial elements deployed to support administrative and operational technologies.

The utility was relatively new and expanding in response to significant development pressure from the expansion of federal agency growth plans that required housing opportunities to support this new level of growth. The utility was highly regarded and building information to support their planning agenda. Growing demand required a regular expansion of infrastructure requirements to be ahead of demand obligations before they overwhelmed the utility. They also operated as a wholesale provider of water supply to various communities such that they effectively insulated themselves from operating normal billing and household supply services that were the responsibility of each community that purchased their water supply.

At the time of the review, the utility was implementing the rollout of a new enterprise-wide management information software. The application would offer improved personnel management, capital program project management, preventive maintenance scheduling, customer service billing, procurement and contract management, year-end financial statements, and so on. Generally, the application was a useful tool and could easily handle the demands of the utility reliant on that software. What was interesting was how the training was being conducted on using the new software. The in-house technology staff manager conducting the training was taxing the mental health of operations and financial staff. He was causing performance challenges that were unnecessary for the staff who would be using the application day after day. In addition, when looking at the capacity and quality of the enterprise application chosen by the utility, it appeared to be more horsepower than the utility needed and/or a Cadillac package when a less robust version would have been suitable. For example, there were only four customers to bill who were receiving bulk water supply to meet daily demand. The extensiveness of the treatment elements was not so complex that a lesser package may have sufficed. The level of complexity the software brought may have contributed to the difficulty of the training and, therefore, a potential reason for the possible frustration of the trainer, who was reported to browbeat the staff each class to the point of tears. Other than that issue, the outcome of the assessment overall was favorable, with some points of recommendation offered. However, I did make a point in the financial section regarding the software rollout. The decision to procure a Cadillac package using a Chevrolet implementation process led by a difficult trainer was building mistrust and frustration as opposed to trust and efficiency realizations inherent with the software. This was a major problem and could ultimately prove to undermine the early benefit of the team using the software. The client officer was reluctant to include this language in the report but acquiesced when I promised to provide a more diplomatic response to this portion of the report for the formal final submittal. It was the reaction of the executive that surprised the client officer. The executive, after reading the report, very much appreciated the candor I provided on the software implementation process and encouraged the client officer not to let this asset go. This is the kind of reality these reports needed if they were going to offer ideas for real improvement and to offer clarity that they were unaware of changing work culture for the better.

Lessons Learned From a Large Water Supply and Treatment Facility Assessment:

Always embrace the role you are given if you are ever assigned to perform an assessment of some kind. Understand the importance of shining light on a problem by asking a broad swath of staff to report on their situation, both good and bad, and what they would like to see changed, improved or not. The lower you go in the organization the more important the information can be for identifying issues to be addressed. Determining if an employee has legitimate concerns or is an example of whining, a shared problem, a policy amendment that needs to be made, or whatever, can be valuable. Remember, the lower echelon staff must live within the rules of the senior leadership team, and offering an avenue for them to access and influence decisions that may improve their working conditions for the better will serve to improve relations between management and staff and encourage acceptance of a shared vision and mission statement of the agency in question.

Assignment: MAJOR CITY UTILITY IN NEW JERSEY

The City's Business Manager pushed the City Council to consolidate the city's independent water and wastewater departments as an efficiency initiative. The current water manager was out of favor and chose to retire rather than be replaced for a lack of confidence vote. He always seemed to act as a high-minded intellectual who led an organization that moved glacially and avoided conflict with city leadership.

The Business Manager was a new player in the city with aspirations to ultimately be Mayor and he needed to build a variety of successful improvements to build his credentials to justify higher office. The water utility had always had a perspective of controversy due to its old system infrastructure that had avoided comprehensive system improvements. New technology could easily reduce maintenance costs and improve operational control of a relatively complex delivery system.

At the same time, the head of wastewater was too new, too friendly, and too much out of the city's organizational culture to be considered for the new Department Head position. The project was to both consolidate the two divisions and serve as a management advisory consultant to the temporary department head out of the

Business Manager's Office. Our focus was to build the policy and administrative guidelines for a joint utility, change the culture of the staff, and focus on reinvestment opportunities. The Water utility was, in many ways, the lead agency of the two and ultimately would serve as the central office for the joint utility. Billing, customer service and engineering already served both utilities out of that space. Essentially, the consolidation was straightforward except for a lack of clear safety training and defined growth opportunities for utility staff. Both utility facilities needed significant updates and rehabilitation. Policies and procedures needed to be refined to reflect improvements suggested by professional organizations (i.e., AWWA, GFOA, WEF). To its benefit, the water utility had an excellent work management procedure that required each service truck to repopulate its materials used for a variety of assigned work orders at the end of their shift and to verify the next morning at the start of the shift that all materials were in place as determined by their standardized guidance sheet. I learned that the City's Finance office, which managed all city agency funds, failed to provide timely monthly revenue and expenditure updates such that spending decisions were delayed due to a lack of clear funds availability. This was resolved with a letter I sent through the interim Manager to the Business Manager. I led regular monthly meetings of all key divisions

119

with the interim manager in attendance to determine the problems they faced daily and to bounce ideas around on how to resolve those problems. This included identifying priorities for capital improvements and how to fund them. This was a real opportunity to build team spirit, promote training ideas they'd like to take advantage of and take ownership of their roles and responsibilities, which we were able to move on now that we were getting better financial data. Communication with the City's Business Manager and Mayor's Office was improving, which allowed contracts to proceed more expeditiously, which led to movement on the appointment of a new manager.

It was an interesting experience for me to work and build an improved working relationship with city offices. I was continually selling progressive strategies to improve and build community confidence and value in the utility sector by updating customer service procedures. This also meant helping to maintain the relationship with a neighboring community that relied on the Water Utility to provide system maintenance and suitable water pressure in a sector of their community that was not connected to the private water company system that served the rest of their community. I received outgoing comments that, somehow, I made leadership look easy just because I always seemed to push against and overcome the old limitations of their glacial decision-making. From my perspective, I was only earning respect by demonstrating leadership skills and confidence in asking for their input to improve the outcome that they understood would be better received by everyone at the utility. I will always argue that success is also built on how well you package your argument for change. What I have found most effective is to first discuss your vision, the expected outcome, and its benefits to the utility and community. Second, you build your case with data that demonstrates the problem and how the planned investment may change that historical trend. Third and final, you write your report like a PhD thesis topic that includes a Thesis, Synthesis, and Anti-Thesis with at least three options. The first option is always your preferred, and the remaining options are presented in order of diminishing returns.

Lessons Learned From Water and Sewer Department Consolidation:

In many ways, this consolidation represented a reset of operational systems, policies, protocols, and mission with the goal of rupturing old systems for new planned programs. Operational metrics had never been identified for measuring work success or progress to justify budget needs. The old practice of avoiding conflict with the City administration gave way to pushing new protocols and business needs regarding budget, finance, procurement, and long-term debt practices. Pulling division leaders into the same room to air their differences, problems, needs, complaints, and desires offered a chance for a whole new organization with a shared vision willing to generate and track new metrics to justify service plans and needs. It also allowed a chance to open the door to realistic training regimens to build growth into titled positions and consideration of a new vehicle replacement strategy that kept working vehicles on the road longer. Assisting with management oversight of the interim manager allowed me to open the person to drive a different leadership style that deviated from what he was told to do by his city bosses. Essentially, learning to value driving an organization as opposed to following directions from those not as well engaged nor informed of day-to-day problems was very satisfying at each "ah ha" moment he experienced.

Assignment: MAJOR CITY ON THE NORTHWEST COAST

The City ran a centralized garage facility that served all municipal departments which would soon include water and wastewater vehicles. My assignment was to focus on bringing water and wastewater into the central garage schedule of repairs without disrupting the priorities given to Police and Fire. The project itself was a dual effort with another consulting group that specialized in centralized garage facilities and my contribution was to support their overall assessment of the existing operation that would eventually include water and wastewater vehicles.

The assumed problem was to correct repetitive failures of vehicle operations to eliminate an endemic weakness in administrative oversight, performance monitoring of mechanic staff, suitability of equipment and materials to meet the objective of the facility, and how they prioritized work. The real question we had was why a centralized operation found it difficult to correct an epidemic of issues with managers who were certified, trained, and paid fairly well. This is where my sleuthing skills that focused on a specific department came into play.

It was clear that the addition of utility vehicles to the central garage schedule would not cause a serious impact on their overall operation. The problem, it turned out, was how well leadership was willing to evolve its organizational operation to include and expand the maintenance schedule to handle the new work demand. The number and type of water and sewer vehicles were not outside the central garages expertise which made the decision to consolidate a reasonable efficiency initiative.

Site visits to their facility and questioning operations staff were useful. I learned that solid waste trucks were not maintained at the central garage but at their own staging site for daily service activities. I learned from the solid waste manager that the Director of the Central Garage regularly overlooked their operation, and they had to do an end run around him to get access to support services. This included running their own work management software, getting contracts with trucking dealerships for warranty work, establishing methods to handle the scheduling of repair requests, and learning how to prioritize their requests, which regularly allowed solid waste trucks to leave unrepaired to meet pickup schedules. Water and wastewater service vehicles were also secondary to all the other city service vehicles (i.e., Police, Fire, Public Works, Engineering, and others) even though they were soon to be maintained at the central garage. Their addition to the Central Garage was to head off possible operations problems of an aging fleet that would need to be put on a formal schedule for replacement. Performance metrics that my firm pulled for me from other community clients defined a real breakdown of coordination and communication, which allowed solid waste trucks an almost daily occurrence of hydraulic fluid leaking on city streets due to delayed repairs. As you would expect, this required regular use of limited labor personnel needed to perform cleanup of those spills. This was a significant black eye for the City staff, who blamed the solid waste garage as opposed to the Director of the overall central garage program, who truly owned this problem. The Director we found was a regular no-show at the office yet was more involved downtown at City Hall. He rarely walked the garage sites nor met regularly to hear complaints or issues needing decisions. My findings were regularly reported to the Assistant City Manager, who oversaw this Department for the City Manager. My report left the Assistant City Manager stumped for a solution. I offered to handle the problem if she would support what I believed was the problem. In essence, I had determined that the Director was approaching retirement and was lessening his involvement in operations to the point that he was leaving too much to chance. I offered to encourage his retirement sooner than later. The Assistant City Manager supported my proposal from a distance since it was nowhere in my scope of work to implement staff changes. But my solution held merit, and she indicated that I could act independently to see if the Director could be encouraged to act in the interest of the City.

I called for a meeting with the Director, Assistant City Manager, and the two senior managers of the two garage sites. I started the meeting with my notebook open for note-taking and informed all that for the first ten minutes, I would close my notebook and the doors to the meeting to have a brief off-the-record discussion. I then gave a broad overview of the leadership problem that was affecting the efficiency and coordination of the centralized garage concept. With the failure of leadership to identify and engage the staff on solutions, I proposed that the obvious solution was a change in leadership and asked him to consider resignation. The Director was not happy with my review, nor did he agree with it. However, when showing him my reports to the Assistant City Manager and the names of staff who I had interviewed with their input, he was frustrated but now stood without a clear safety net since the Assistant City Manager was quiet. I offered again that it would be preferable if he submitted his resignation to retire six months from now, providing time to mentor and train a potential candidate to replace him. The other option was to face a potential performance review and subsequent termination based on the material arranged in front of him. I asked the Assistant City Manager if he could have 24 hours to respond before a performance review would be recommended. She agreed, and I reopened my notebook and proceeded to report formally my findings and recommendations. The outcome was favorable, and the Director submitted his resignation letter, as suggested, the next day. The Assistant City Manager had been extremely nervous but was grateful for how well I handled that very difficult situation and that there was a real opportunity to improve this sector of the city budget. My firm was not necessarily happy that I pulled that stunt without making them aware, but they acknowledged the extremely positive report they received on the outcome of the whole project with my name mentioned prominently as a real asset instrumental in the outcome. Again, my willingness to take a risk where I saw an obvious outcome could have been ruinous to my future if the whole affair had not gone so well. However, it was always my sentiment that my role as a consultant was to demonstrate both new ways of looking at their organization as well as demonstrating what a true leader should be promoting as a vision for success. My firm acknowledged my rogue style of acting and that I should be aware that they weren't necessarily comfortable with my actions. But in the end, I repeatedly demonstrated a difference that made me one of the stronger Senior Project Managers in the Management Consulting group.

Lessons Learned From Central Garage Operational Assessment:

A graceful exit by a long-term manager from a position of critical importance for emergency responders and daily required vehicle operations to meet the business schedules of an engaged public is and can be a big deal depending on how those remaining have been mentored correctly to maintain and sustain a strong business model. In this case, a forced exit with grace achieved the same end and allowed closure that opened the door to creating an improved relationship affected by the change in leadership. This is the value of performance metrics that can measure over time the success and weaknesses of an operation that must meet key performance benchmarks for the benefit and protection of the public. The metrics were few at the start of this evaluation, but a broad list was introduced with the change in new leadership that the deposed manager helped establish.

Assignment: SMALL COUNTY ON LAKE PONTCHARTRAIN

I did a brief stint for a locale on Lake Pontchartrain where there was a preponderance of properties, residential and commercial, that relied on septic systems to manage their on-site organic waste treatment. The situation was troubling in that every property along every road had a storm trench, generally soil, not concrete, open to the sky that handled the high amount of normal rainfall in the area. The trenches drained ultimately to the lake, flushing both storm and septic-influenced organic material coming out of the septic systems that were rather shallowly built. The incidence of high organic values from runoff near the outfalls of the various storm drains to the lake had come to the attention of the EPA. EPA notified the county that the lake's failing water quality would require action that would push the development of a wastewater management solution and would shift the Parish to a wastewater treatment program. It was our recommendation that they prepare a solid proposal to correct a known problem before the EPA got involved. This would allow them to establish a solution they could control and potentially afford within a time frame that the EPA would accept since they were already pushing change that met the EPA's concerns.

The project I was given was to produce a management document for the creation of a multi-departmental organization that pulled together the existing Engineering, Public Works, Parks, solid waste, and a new utility program overseeing stormwater management and wastewater treatment. The document I produced provided a comprehensive review of the fiscal and operational conditions that I found. It also outlined a proposal to consolidate and create a corporate structure and work culture that cross-trained labor to handle multi-agency needs and pursued the latest technologies in treatment. This approach allowed the Parish to build capacity with a gradual impact on ongoing budget demands, which included the issuance of long-term debt needed to install wastewater pipelines and construct a new wastewater treatment facility. Each division in the organization was defined along with performance metrics to measure progress over time. I was able to pull together all my experience and promote a relatively streamlined operation that took advantage of economies of scale and a utility rate structure that was progressive for generating maintenance reserves for long-term sustainability.

Lessons Learned From New Departmental Model:

Creating a new departmental structure, division by division, with a defined management philosophy and new workday expectations to coordinate, along with the procurement of appropriate key equipment needs, is a rare opportunity to get it right the first time. Expectations of the client were high, and the budget impact had to be realistic to allow the packaging of the proposal to sell itself. The key was to query and question existing division managers and their field staff to gain a real understanding of what they could accept and easily implement. Funds for training had to be part of the package along with work management software to build the beginnings of an asset management system.

Separately, I have found from my experience running a utility that driving a solution early that addresses most of the key areas of concern identified by a regulatory body overseeing your operation, both state and federal, provides an opportunity to control the outcome in your favor. Developing a plan ahead of a ruling by them requires action be taken and opens the door to a mutual understanding which demonstrates: i) your agency is committed to making the necessary changes along with the necessary funding, ii) the agency demonstrates a clear vision that mirrors the regulators expectations, and iii) the agency further demonstrates a willingness to commit the time needed to put together the necessary documentation (i.e., strategic plans, revised master plans, what-if scenarios, and staging exercises) to build the foundation for movement towards a desired outcome. This approach offered an avenue for building a degree of trust that didn't exist before and allowed them to negotiate more favorable terms that were easier to manage.

Assignment: INDEPENDENT COUNTRY IN SOUTH AFRICA

It is my belief that the reason I was tasked with a troubling assignment to a South African nation was due to my history of managing difficult organizational concerns. The assignment was to correct a serious communication problem between the head of the party from my firm running the design and construction project and the executive officer assigned by the national legislature to oversee the project to protect their interests. The grant-funded project was to build a new water retention dam that would serve a new water treatment facility to supply potable water to a large portion of the capital city. There were five international donor entities funding the work with differing submittal guidelines needed to request reimbursement for project activities, engineering, and construction. Knowing each donor's requirement and following it to the letter was critical because some wanted receipts for reimbursement that matched planned expenditures, some wanted a request of quarterly spending needs to receive funding upfront to move forward each quarter, and some wanted a comprehensive spending plan where progress payment requests were submitted as work proceeded. The bottom line was that no funding would move forward unless there was a clear demonstration of coordination within the program office that met the deliverables demanded by each donor entity.

Getting to this client's location was an interesting transit. After a 15-hour flight, I spent the night in Johannesburg at a residence for expats having drinks and dinner with other consulting professionals. They informed me the transition from Apartheid to a more democratic governmental system hadn't been clean and efficient. This was a lot to take in. Johannesburg needed professionals like me to take over activities across the government to correct the problems that started when the prior government left, and the new government pushed untrained, unskilled, unaware, and corrupt individuals to take on all the roles of professional government.

This turned out to be a good segway into what I was getting into in this small client State. The State is water-rich, small in size like Rhode Island, where they relied heavily on the sales of water to South Africa for revenue. They also relied on cheap mass labor groups to finalize well-known corporate brand materials for transport to the US and other nations (i.e., GAP, Sylvania bulbs, and others). There is also a high infection rate of HIV, about 1/2 of the country, which impacts the weak condition of the local population and why the new water source was needed to expand access to an improved and treated water supply.

What I found at the project office with all of this going on around us was troubling, to say the least. The Executive Officer was from an earlier time when the British ran most of the foreign project assignments. He attempted to run the operation from a godlike perch with tea time in the afternoon. In many ways, he was disconnected from what was happening at the office. The Finance Officer was English as well who oversaw a French World Bank funding software written in a French operating language that he didn't understand. That one software was totally unsuitable for meeting the submittal requirements of the other four donor entities, yet it was the only software he had. The Grants Manager, a local matron with a degree in Accounting from Oxford, was fully capable of preparing grant submittals, but the documentation she needed couldn't be produced by the French funding software. That relied on the Finance Office accounting staff to populate a database that the Finance Officer couldn't run. On top of that, the other donor entities didn't follow the World Bank model, and therefore, a different software was needed to prepare submittals. The source of the daily work assignments came through the Head of Party which he then fed to the accounting staff. It was at this time I learned that the Head of Party was building an interface to its North Carolina office to run a separate project software stateside as a backstop that would be able to generate documentation needed to satisfy grant submittal requirements. However, the information, model of format submittals, and responses from donors still needed to come through accounting, then Finance, to the Grant Manager's Office. The funding situation for the project was in a perilous state since a grant submittal hadn't been made for more than a year due to the coordination problem that was not happening. My firm's Head of Party was very concerned about the success of the project. He was at a loss on how to correct the problem. I had been given thirty days to correct it.

I immediately established my role as the lead fixer for this project on the first day. I quickly informed the Executive Officer that I would be shaking things up in the office without his permission and expected him to cooperate with all my findings. He was a bit put out, but he acquiesced since he did know there was a problem that he wasn't managing. I then learned that the Grants Manager was considered a high person in the State's culture with status as a matron of her family. Since two of the Finance staff that captured expenditure data and managed project budgets were her daughters, they were restricted from her office and could only submit information she needed through the Finance Officer. This was the same with the firm's database donor information that would be coming from North Carolina.

My solution was straightforward. I told the daughters that during their mother's lunch break, about 1 ½ hours, they should enter her office, without her knowing, to get the data sheets they needed for each donor model to capture status report guidelines, to fill out the required data submittals that could then be sent to the firm Finance Office for submittal to the Grant's office. They jumped on it, and within a week, they started submitting donor documents for reimbursement. There was also a requirement to implement a document management protocol so that project activity and critical project documents could be tracked and organized using an electronic database format. That required walking two locals through the program implementation training regimen to organize a year's worth of paper documents that were piling up. There was also an element of engineering oversight that required fieldwork to build a knowledge base of the basalt deposits that would be used to build a dam when the firm's engineer came in from Vietnam. That information fed the preparation of a construction document to build the dam using local materials. The engineering documents, plans, criteria, measurements, and so on were constantly being updated, and the Executive Officer was suspicious of the quality of the output such that he brought in a retired friend, at a very high wage, to second guess the engineering staff where he never found a flaw. Alleviating the suspicious nature of the Executive Officer's team monitoring the engineering group was a challenge, but regular meetings began to soften his ire through open communication and clarity of responsibilities. Leading these meetings was an art form.

I ended my stay in the nation/state office at a meeting with all staff. I described my findings in full which the Executive took issue with until I showed him my notes documented by his own team. I also threatened to report my findings to the State Legislative Committee that oversaw the project, which was not in the loop on the funding problems that the Executive Officer was having with the project. I stated that he had to agree to support and maintain the changes I introduced so that the project would be back on track within the month. The client manager back in the States who oversaw the firm's project relationship with the State government called me and affirmed the reinstatement of cash flow from all the donor entities. He was a little concerned when he spoke with the Executive Officer about how I had mistreated him, but based on the success of getting movement restarted, he was more than appreciative that I had pressed appropriately where I needed to. About a year later, I was called to make a second trip to reaffirm the project protocols, which were slipping due to the Executive Officer attempting to reestablish his control, which he always had but managed poorly.

Lessons Learned From an International Client:

Walking into a cold situation can be an enlightening experience that forewarning could have muddled and jaded the real story on the ground. My initial meeting with the Head of Party, a member of my firm, gave me a suitable warning to measure my risk-taking. What I learned at the introductory meeting with the Executive Officer suggested my method of action. My first and only question was, "What did he know to be the problems of the project?" He could not describe the weaknesses without admitting he didn't control the situation. With this understanding, you first acknowledge his role but demonstrate your independence because control was critical and funding issues must be managed consistently and this wasn't the case. Learning the cultural roadblocks is the lotion for smoothing the waters between differing societal norms. Understanding the limitations of key players is also central to overcoming problems in communication. At this stage, making a decision that leads to a small win is critical. Making a subsequent big win is dramatic and gives an outsider the power to influence what they never would have had without the new information. Working from that success allows the players of each distinct group, of which there were three, to open their books and share their information. Having launched a funding solution, it provided a chance to open the protocols for submission of the required data deliverables that had been tightly held. A workaround served to introduce the opening for change, supporting the donor's justification for reimbursement.

The situation on the ground in that community was a bit unsettling and very concerning due to the high incidence of HIV in the general population. Walking was the preferred method of transport around the city, but the chances for contact with the local population were very high and worrying. Foreign travel is always a challenging pursuit until you learn the local customs and safe protocols for movement.

Assignment: LARGE CITY NEAR LAKE HURON

The water authority for the City is an old and dated operation. The City had a historic story of past glory with the present reality of being forgotten and declining in national status. This was the condition of the authority that held a prominent role in trying to effectively serve a community that was large, with neighborhoods experiencing severe neglect and service priorities earmarked for reactive support where problems accumulated rather than being driven by preventive maintenance practices due to a lack of funding. Our role was to perform an operational and fiscal assessment of the water utility. The size of the operation was broad and included a water source facility from Lake Huron providing a large percentage of the city's water supply that was piped a significant distance to serve the metropolitan area. As with other large water utilities, they shared the same problems of age and maintenance deferral. With the falling population trend in the city, the flexibility of the utility to generate funds required them to be very strategic in what maintenance and repair they could do. We were able to offer guidelines for targeted funding to resurrect the utility, however, a slowly developing rebirth within the city would be the time for pursuing the bulk of the recommendations we provided.

It was clear that the city's utility operations were stretched and required ongoing support that included both funding and new leadership talent at the middle management level to help prepare a master plan and/or a strategic plan that would work in tandem with the city's own master plan and redevelopment efforts.

The assignment required us to travel to a wide variety of facilities that were in operation and allowed an understanding of the level of service required to meet demand expectations. It was obvious that they were in a period of reduced demand. However, the understanding was that they wanted to get things in order during the lull in demand so that they could manage the expected resurgence of city redevelopment.

Lessons Learned From a Water Department Assessment:

The City had a long and storied past with a declining population, elimination and clearing of large sectors of the residential community due to job losses, and the relocation of manufacturing to overseas low-cost labor locations. The problem everyone faced was the reality that the infrastructure could not be reduced in size and extent due to the broad footprint within the City's legally required service area. Funding from the City was inadequate for repairing what was needed to shift the department into a new era. We understood that starting discussions to build a strategy with plans and implementation scenarios that could be rolled out once funding was realized could work. But time was their nemesis, and despite a talented leadership team, redevelopment activity was necessary sooner than later.

Assignment: LARGE WASTEWATER UTIL-ITY IN MID-ATLANTIC STATE

The wastewater authority represents the coordination of nine communities to receive wastewater treatment services at one centralized regional facility. The scope of this entity has been a long-term success, with a bump in the road related to a potentially significant capital upgrade, which had the utility not realizing its best course of action. My assignment was to evaluate each of the participating communities' combined annual daily flow contributions, wastewater, and stormwater, look at FOG (fats, oil, and grease) impacts contributed by each community, and determine how much each community would then be obligated to pay or amend their local service rates to cover their portion of a capacity treatment upgrade due to both new regulations and projected population impacts for the next twenty-five years.

It was interesting that I was never given an opportunity to meet and discuss the parameters of the assessment that would feed a decision on the size of the required expansion with members of each community, council members, engineering, or operations staff. I had to use the information that was provided to the regional utility for making all of my determinations, which essentially placed a strait jacket on findings and did not allow me to gain opinions on what possible considerations each community might be open to discuss, consider, support, or deny.

At the outset, I was informed that the Council member representatives from each participating community were relatively closed-minded to progressive approaches that might affect rates even though flow data systems installed independently by each community defined their own contribution needing treatment.

I approached the capital infrastructure expansion question from two directions:

1) The direct relationship of rate increases apportioned based on the projected facility expansion aligned with the direct daily flow average contribution by each member community.

2) The benefit of controlling projected flow contribution with implementation of flow control measures affecting stormwater diversion using a variety of means (i.e., flow capture using impoundments to slow flow release over time, which eliminated storm surge; installing flow weirs in collection mains to slow flow surge; the capture and reuse of stormwater for irrigation; the introduction of updated FOG control measures; or possible recharge of shallow aquifer sources (used by some commercial interests) that would reduce their apportionment of capital costs affecting their community rates. The

approach is to downsize the size of the capital expansion based on lower daily flow projections per customer/city.

I went on to prepare a map of each community's drainage system, the locations of each community's discharge points to the interceptor system owned by the Authority, the location of each flowmeter registering flows into the interceptor pipe, and the possible sections of interceptor that would need widening or a parallel pipeline installed to carry the additional projected flows. The review of each community's FOG control requirements, or lack thereof, was also evaluated to determine the level of impact it might have on the elimination of a major contributor of toxic elements that were impacting the potential regulatory enhancements built into the expansion. I then prepared a PowerPoint for presentation to the Authority's Board demonstrating the benefits and weaknesses of the two approaches. The Board chose to follow option one despite real opportunities to downsize flow contributions suggested in the various communities. The reason is an unwillingness to raise taxes to pay for the capital amendments to their individual collection systems and to try something new and, in today's terms, green. The need to amend and update FOG control measures that included the expanded use of grease interceptors, city health inspections, and enforcement also contributed to the decision to defer to a shared treatment solution.

There was also a political reason that could expose each Council person to singularly promoting a tax increase that would not be well received by the larger community. City Council members were already suffering under high tax complaint pressures.

Lessons Learned From a Multi-City Wastewater Collection System Assessment:

I was told by a consultant representing one of the communities that I should not take their decision too hard even though the Option 2 proposal was really the correct one for them. Political realism will always be the master over common sense proposals if your future is to remain in politics for the long term. Rogue politicians open to promoting a new direction are refreshing, rare, and, in many cases, short-lived. This may be the case until the measure being addressed becomes of greater consequence than following the old approach of a shared pain (option 1) over an individual cost approach (option 2) with long-term savings after several years of investment, which may take longer than the council person's term in office.

Assignment: LARGE CITY ON LAKE ERIE

The regional Sewer Authority operated independently of the water utility for the metropolitan area. Like other older communities discussed earlier, it shared the same problem of disinvestment and deferral of maintenance. The project being implemented was to populate a newly procured work management system to roll out an asset management (AM) program that gave them the justification for new investment. The work involved establishing a new management philosophy that invested in both capital and workforce, producing new training opportunities, amending job titles, reorganizing staging sites for work teams, updating to a centralized timecard system for those same staging sites, and building long-term master plan updates for the various districts that made up the metropolitan area. The rollout was straightforward and successful and represented a significant learning initiative for operations personnel. There was also a major effort being made to mentor a younger generation of junior and/or middle management staff who were being trained to oversee the use and functionality of the new AM protocols for reporting and budget management. The push to implement was transformative for the organization that had relied on outdated methods for managing a large, complicated program that had delayed introducing many state-of-the-art practices well established for the utility industry.

The meetings with field personnel and operations chiefs allowed us to open the conversation to new planning concepts and scheduling capabilities that they had never considered nor had the capacity to use. The idea of prioritizing repairs based on criticality and condition, which could ultimately extend the useful life of key assets, was new to them. Repairing components based on a deliberate preventive maintenance strategy suggested by a manufacturer or by the staff with experience attending to those pieces of equipment was a whole new perspective for them to take in. It was clear that they embraced the potential of the AM effort and how to take full advantage of the software being populated which used a hierarchical approach for comparative assessments of like assets. This would give them the justification to standardize equipment based on actual operational experience with the lowest-cost long-lived assets.

Lessons Learned From a Large Asset Management (AM) System Roll Out:

If leadership and operations staff are open and accepting of changes from the outset that give them a real upgrade in overall program satisfaction and development, the chance of success is dramatic. The initial meetings that were held to introduce the plans for the AM program were led by a young senior manager from the city who saw the opportunity offered and the benefit to their own growth as a viable outcome. Rare, but it does happen that you can find a leader who puts the organization first and drives means and methods for change by being the voice of that movement. The regulatory environment was also on the side of the city, which was driving consideration of formal action if changes weren't made in both treatment improvements and collection system updates. The city saw it may be a better investment if they kept control of what improvements they would make as opposed to what EPA might propose to achieve the same end. This represents a negotiated strategy over the imposition of a directive.

Transitioning Back to the Public Sector

LARGE CITY UTILITY ON NORTHWEST COAST

Agency Description:

The semi-independent water supply, sewer collection, and solid waste collection department, which provides City-wide coverage and transmission support to the County for wastewater treatment, was a model national example of asset management on the surface with a weak organizational and administrative structure hidden underneath. The size and complication of the community were extensive due to distant water supply and land management requirements, salmon run protection areas, large water storage and distribution systems, wastewater collection and pumping system facilities, protection of key environmental properties, and the handling of solid waste and train transport. All required expansive oversight responsibilities.

Leaving the consulting firm was not by choice, but due to a period when there had been a downturn in work. Thinning costly, even valuable personnel was necessary to transition into the new reality. That reality included the firm acquiring a new company to expand the footprint of services that had synergies with our existing program of services. After a brief sojourn looking for new work, landing on the Northwest coast should have been a major opportunity. My new boss hired me because we had done seminars together in the past where we trained area utilities on the concept, value, implementation requirements, and protocols needed to shift towards an asset management (AM) philosophy. Little did I know what I would find at this new work assignment. What I did find was a utility with a long-standing understanding of being a leader in AM when, in reality, they were only just instituting the basics of an AM program.

AM realistically requires a global perspective and a comprehensive utility-wide program affecting all areas of operation and management to build an efficient, timely, and forward-thinking professional entity. The Utility was well known to be a progressive AM enterprise through presentations at various national conferences. What was interesting on my first day was what my boss told me in private. He informed me that once I looked under the hood of the Utility's AM program, there wasn't much to find, and it was true.

Despite the significant investment the Utility had made in new software training managers in the subject which included sending staff to Australia who is the known leader in AM, my finding was the utility had not even completed the first requirement. This is to identify all the critical assets owned by the utility and populate a database a CMMS (computerized maintenance management software) system with all key asset data using a hierarchy for comparative asset assessments to establish a process for enhanced preventive maintenance and scheduled replacement planning. The fallacy was that this finding came to me after they had implemented their stated plan over the prior ten years.

For example, they had finally completed covering seven large in-ground water reservoirs with ball fields, soccer fields, and parks built over them. The Utility took advantage of significant rolling terrain which allowed them to minimize the reliance on standpipes and water towers. What was interesting is that I found they failed to include any of them in the database. The same with a new $1.5 billion solid waste facility which had taken 10 years to design and build. Of greater interest was my finding that when they procured the new CMMS system, senior management chose to discount the need to create an asset hierarchy that allows a user to compare and contrast assets across the agency's dispersed set of facilities. Measurement of criticality against condition assessments that drove prioritization decisions had never been done nor captured on the system. This was a significant oversight. The work management system identified assets with a unique asset number. However, the unique assets associated with each site were dumped into one common bucket description without a maintenance plan assigned to each unique asset group or component within that group (e.g., water reservoirs, wastewater pumping stations, pressure reduction vaults, and others). This was the same approach the Utility used to identify assets on the agency's balance sheet such that when they replaced an asset, rather than identifying the specific section of water main replacement, for example, they just grabbed a water main value in the larger pool of pipeline assets and subtracted an average value of original investment rather than the actual depreciated value of investment by type of pipe and repair efforts over time. Accuracy apparently was not their goal.

The only initiative they could brag about was their case study work associated with capital projects above a specified value. The value engineering effort of these case studies is to ensure the best solution was chosen to address the identified problem. But in many cases, the expense of performing this work was more costly than actual design and construction. Part of the reason was the design evaluation was given to a third-party consultant to perform the what-if exercises and then they were allowed to design the final approved alternative. The design engineers working at the utility were never given design work for these case studies. Essentially, a gravy train to the consultant community.

It is not surprising that the ineptness of senior leadership allowed for this level of dysfunction. For example, the Deputy Director believed he was a solid model of leadership capability even though he regularly made mistakes dealing with union staff contractual guidelines, which undermined management's position. He allowed junior staff to bypass their immediate boss to communicate with him directly when they had a complaint rather than working out their disagreements before they rose to senior leadership. It was because they were well known to him as being long-term employees and were friends which created broken working relationship conditions. This made enforcement of more senior leadership directives difficult to manage if the employee didn't want to do what he/she was told to do by their immediate supervisor.

During regular meetings of senior management, they heard about progress on capital activities and requests for approval to amend projects where circumstances had changed, and new funding may be needed. One time, while attending a manager's meeting to discuss how to schedule the use of several new street sweepers with brush, water, and suction elements. This new equipment would assist with addressing stormwater management concerns where storm drains potentially captured toxic materials (i.e., Brake filings, oil droplets, rubber tire elements) from road networks. Street sweepers could be used to flush and capture these materials. Capturing the toxins in their onboard tank beds for sanitary disposal rather than allowing them to be flushed into the regional lake would avoid adding to the exposure of inert materials harming the water quality of the lake and reduce a major concern of the Federal EPA. Someone suggested that a consultant be hired to schedule the use of those vehicles. I raised my hand and offered to do the scheduling rather than spending the money on a consultant since I was familiar with what was needed. Everyone laughed except the Operations Director. Someone stated that it just wasn't that easy. My reply was simple. "Oh, it's easy, alright. However, what you have just indicated is that you have given away all of your management control rights over your unionized operations staff. Basically, you cannot tell your union employees, the hours they can and will work, including evenings and weekends, which is what's needed." Everyone stared at me with that uneasy feeling that they had been found out, and then they all got up in mass and left the meeting except for the Operations

Director. He stated that "you are exactly right, and he had been try-ing to fix the problem for three years." The new union contract was presently in dispute, and this was one of the issues that he was at-tempting to reestablish.

Over the course of my data discovery, I learned that the sensitiv-ity of senior managers to accept pushbacks and/or advice for deci-sions they may have made was not taken well, which was driving a wedge of frustration within the senior administrative ranks. The Mayor and Council of the city were both second guessing and sup-porting the direction of master planning and strategic planning by the Utility. This was demonstrated when a division head over solid waste rate-setting decisions forgot to include the cost impact of maintaining a new solid waste handling facility into a declared five-year rate lock proposal recently adopted by the city as part of the Utility's strategic plan following extensive public hearings. As a re-sult, the city had to agree to step in to cover the budget impact until the next rate amendment, but they warned of repercussions if this level of weak oversight happened again.

During one of my field visits to the operations district office to discuss what changes needed to be introduced to the data collection methodology needed for populating the database effectively, I found an unexpected opportunity. While speaking with the database leader, I learned of a Clerk who was capturing all the work orders for all three utilities. The details she captured included field repairs and maintenance activity, the hours projected, and actual time expensed based on the number of staff assigned to each work order. She had previously worked for a private contractor and had used the information to price projects for client billing. The utility never used any of her data for its own tracking and cost estimating. The data could have been used to determine optimum staffing needs, time and staff projections, and setting budget estimates by month or season where activity varied based on weather patterns. It was all there and available but never incorporated into the database for planning and scheduling. This was a major oversight.

At the same time as this prior finding, the utility hired a new planning analyst for operations, and I proposed to him to become a Planner/Scheduler who would incorporate and use the Clerk's work order tracking data. He liked the suggestion and proposed this strategy to his immediate boss. When I left the agency, I never knew if he was successful.

What is also interesting is that senior management didn't learn from this experience. They continued to move ahead as if the old ways were the best avenue of choice. Even as I found other examples of poor management and shortsighted decision making.

158

A good example was what I found during my standard review of a new project proposal scheduled to receive a case study assignment. The utility had failed to include the cost of one of the most expensive stormwater management projects they would ever build. It was a simple inquiry I made to the project engineer leading this assignment, who, upon review of the recently adopted strategic plan, found no listing that included nor funded the long-term debt for the project. I reported this to the Deputy Director who was shocked again as much as the prior oversight of the solid waste facility. The oversight came through the same person for both who was never reprimanded nor demoted. Shortly thereafter, the Deputy Director put that same person in charge of my division following the resignation of my former boss, essentially assuring the Peter Principle was met and, in this case, exceeded. The Deputy Director went on to give lectures to interested Utility staff on the leadership principles he followed, which I found to be disreputable and egregious.

Another example of leadership weakness was when I was drawn into a developing problem initiative associated with grease entering the sewer collection system from the failure of city inspectors not requiring and enforcing installation and maintenance standards for grease interceptor systems. The utility needed to determine who was truly responsible financially for controlling and performing

159

maintenance and/or corrective surgery to the piping system due to upstream contributors, primarily from restaurants, causing a grease blockage downstream. Having had experience dealing with this issue, I was intrigued when the division head dealing with this problem asked to meet with me and discuss the subject from an AM point of view. Once learning of my history of creating guidelines and implementing a viable strategy that pulled together a coordinated multi-agency solution of City/County health departments, code enforcement, restaurant health inspection, and televised collection system data capture protocols, I was asked to attend a strategy session. I found out there were a large number of interested parties who would be building the Utility's action plan. It was informative that the division head allowed the city's lawyers to take the lead on what they determined was a format to follow. With no one else raising concerns out of a group of thirty, I said that at all future meetings, members of the County Health Department and City Building Code division should be in attendance to establish the coordinated protocol for adopting new guidelines for enforcement purposes and building permit requirements of FOG (fats, oils, and grease) contributors. These guidelines would be backed by formal action of those bodies. I emphasized that the County and City had control through permit and building code guidelines for restaurants and such, which the Utility could not enforce without their involvement. The lawyers disagreed that it required their involvement at this time, which I pressed and got the division head to rule that at the next meeting, they would be asked to attend to determine if I was right or not. Ultimately, I was proven right, and with the embarrassment of my action, the lawyers asked that I no longer attend unless needed. It was interesting that the manager in charge of this effort continued to review all progress with me prior to gaining the larger committee's approval. Again, the sensitivity of common-sense actions on perceived knowledge wonks further demonstrated the dysfunction of the senior leadership team.

Returning to Asset Management activities, I went on to build a draft hierarchy model for a majority of assets owned by the utility, by department, by division, by category of purpose, and finally by asset group. I even went so far as to put together a PowerPoint presentation for senior management, the Engineering Group, and key Operations staff detailing my findings and next steps to implement. Before I gave it, I did a practice run with my immediate staff who found the message accurate in the telling but more so embarrassing and punitive in the story. "I would hurt people's feelings." I essentially outlined a comprehensive picture of the deliberate failure to build an AM structure by senior management even as I proposed a multi-year solution to get the Utility on track with this program that they had been pursuing for ten years. I never had the chance to give the presentation because of the backlash I'd get from senior managers who saw themselves as unique and all-knowing, even though they were too smart, too sensitive, and too shallow.

I did have a chance to speak with the Finance and Budget staff of the utility and learned that they were not given the option to perform field work other than attend public hearings before community groups to answer budget questions. An explanation of my work history and the value of learning a field perspective to improve their budget analyses was well received by my staff contacts. However the division head did not like my intrusion into her domain and dispelled the importance of it without disputing the evidence I offered. This was despite my insistence that a field perspective would build a bridge for endorsing the asset management philosophy I was hoping to implement.

As I've indicated earlier, no good deed goes unpunished. At this point, I was asked to leave at the end of my probationary period by the Deputy Director because he considered me a disruption in the leadership team. He tried to argue that I challenged the well-practiced old narrative that saw major gaps in the implementation of their management philosophy. Senior leaders disliked my independent initiative, whereas everyone below management saw me as someone who finally understood what the AM strategy should have been all these years.

Lessons Learned From Strategic Asset Management (AM) Effort:

I was the third person to hold the Strategic AM position, and I left just as the others before me left under a cloud of mistrust by senior management because we were promoting a direction that did not coincide with the plans of senior management that wrapped control around themselves. AM, by practice, pushes an element of decision-making down to the field staff, who must evaluate asset conditions and determine if the schedule of preventive maintenance was adequate, could be slowed down, or increased in frequency due to operating conditions. This could change on a seasonal basis, which would be noted in the CMMS system, impacting scheduling requirements. Ultimately, reporting protocols provide data to measure progress and success. This approach would have left senior management with less hands-on control, which they couldn't abide as suitable to their own interests. I left the utility disillusioned that there was such a disconnect between senior leadership and lower echelon staff who embraced my findings yet were threatening to senior control and order.

AN ISLAND IN THE WESTERN PACIFIC OCEAN

At this point and after another brief sojourn looking for work, I was called by a former colleague to consider applying for an executive role on a Pacific island running their water and wastewater utility. I did apply and was invited to an on-site interview with the Board. It was an interesting interview process because the Board chose to test my hands-on management and operational evaluation assessment skills. Essentially, after a brief interview and introductory meetings with senior staff, they gave me four hours to ride with operations staff to visit their facilities, locales of operation, work sites, treatment facilities, and so on, and then report back my findings. My report to them astounded their expectations. I found numerous issues of concern: poor field practices, regulatory control breaches, poor inventory monitorization of parts utilization, poor vehicle maintenance, outstanding billing payments by major customers without a plan to correct the failure to pay, and no multi-year plan for tracking and planning capital construction needs which were normally done in response to a failure. The Board was impressed to the point that they wanted to retain me for the position, but the decision required full Board approval, and one member was unavailable that week. To be brief, I was not chosen because the missing Board member wanted an engineer for the position regardless of the findings I had identified, which demonstrated a real weakness in operational integrity.

Ultimate Destination and Agency Description:

An independent water, sewer, and power utility with a seven-member board operating on three of thirteen islands defined as a commonwealth that is a creature of the Territorial State Legislature which operated outside its control but with the support of the United States Environmental Protection Agency (USEPA) and other federal agencies. However, independence also required the support of a state Rate Setting Commission, appointed by the Governor, to approve any rate amendments and debt obligations for each service entity.

Ultimately, I landed on an island Commonwealth, a territory of the United States, serving as the Deputy Executive Director of a Water, Sewer, and Power utility for the next five years. The situation I found were examples of serious weaknesses in service quality; a weak and inexperienced senior management team, professional compromise by key staff, legislative intrusion by the island government over the independent utility, and a dated infrastructure for all three departmental systems that serve an island population of 50,000 and tourist numbers totaling, on average, 50,000 per month. The by-laws worked against the progressive potential of the utility because of the requirement that rate amendments had to be proposed and approved by a governmental rate commission appointed by the Governor. The rate commission hadn't been active nor populated for more than eight years. It also required the commission to hire an independent consultant to evaluate the proposed rate submittal. A conflict existed with this appointment because the utility was obligated to pay for their services even though they were working potentially at cross purposes to the in-house finance team. The last rate hearing cost the utility more than $1 million just for the consultant, not including their own costs to argue for the changes.

I had initially applied to be the Executive Director of the organization, but my lack of experience in power generation and distribution had the legal staff suggest I take the Deputy role since I was strong on water and sewer, which was the primary assignment of that position. Power was to remain with the Acting Executive Director who came from power and was ultimately given the title following my appointment. I found the senior management team to be relatively young and inexperienced, with limited exposure to the realities of mainland utility management practices. As a result, my role would end up being a mentor to each division of administration and overseeing major improvements in prioritization to fund a significant change in the direction to be taken to invest in broad infrastructure requirements.

A major assignment for me included the need to address Federal Stipulated Order #2 which had been imposed on the utility's water and sewer departments by a Federal District Court Judge for Region 9. With the acceptance of federal grant funds from the Federal Department of Environmental Protection (EPA) and the Federal Department of Interior (DOI), they demanded greater oversight in the delivery of services and the funding of capital improvements to island facilities. There were 69 stipulated requirements under this Order, and only 23 had been completed. The master plan had not been presented to the public for their input to gain final EPA approval. I prioritized the closure of all remaining orders. I was able to complete all but four within my five years, and those had been set up for final action by the time I left. Part of the success in completing the orders involved gaining the confidence of the Federal Judge from Region 9, who visited the island every six months. We had to report to the Federal Court to present our progress and to gain his approval of actionable items.

One event cemented the confidence and respect I earned from the Federal Judge and why I was able to greatly expand federal funding for the various island facilities. The first time I met the Judge in court, I offered a tour of the relevant facilities we had identified for improvement to match the strategic plan and vision for improving system durability and sustainability. The Judge traveled with a legal aid, an EPA attorney, and a Federal District Court attorney who worked through the Chief Engineer at the utility. The improvements included expanding water service from eight hours per day to twenty-four hours each day, which had never happened in the history of the island. As part of the tour, I required field staff to answer questions from the Judge rather than from the Chief Engineer who had a separate agenda and was continually undermining my plans. One of my initiatives was to enhance field and operations staff through training, mentoring, and participation in planning activities. The Judge was surprised at the broad understanding of field personnel to long-term planning efforts, the purpose for making the new changes being implemented, and the confidence they demonstrated in answering his questions. The tour ended in a conference room with a large map of the island, where I gave a one-hour presentation of what my findings had been and where the utility was going in the future with the steps I was taking to focus on a clear set of priorities. The Judge quietly told me, towards the conclusion of the presentation, that "that was one of the best presentations of purpose he had ever heard." I learned two days later when the Judge, federal attorneys, and the EPA representative had flown back to their offices on the mainland. The Judge had been extremely upset with his legal team and EPA because they had lied to him about the real issues happening on the island based on my presentation. He demanded they fund and support my plans with no complaints or heads would roll.

The infrastructure of the three departments was truly on life support on all three islands the utility served. On the main island:

- Power generation has two power plants totaling 146 MW using diesel fired 5 MW mechanical generators that were more than 45 years old and did not have any automated systems. Everything was manual. They had exceeded life expectancy by five or more years but were still in service. The distribution system relied on wooden power poles for the backbone of their power network with one primary underground segment that served a small area and the international airport.

- Wastewater has two treatment plants serving 50 percent of the population, with the balance covered by septic systems that were affecting the various aquifers serving the island with elevated levels of nitrates and regularly causing red flag warnings along the local beaches. Secondary treatment systems were compromised by insufficient maintenance of key systems due to a lack of knowledgeable talent overseeing maintenance operations.

- Water was undrinkable on the island due to high chloride content due to aquifers with an insufficient depth to avoid pumping salt water due to the proximity of the saltwater interface that lay below the freshwater zone. The effects of the cone of influence from pumping cavitation could not be avoided. As a result, the population used the non-potable water for showers, washing, laundry, and such but not to drink, which was only available 8 hours a day. Drinking water was provided by private companies with desalination units sold through grocery stores. The resorts had their own desal facilities, which they used for their property requirements and clientele. In addition, the island was losing 65% of its supply through leaks, bad joints, cracked pipes and water theft. The original piping serving sectors of the island had illegal taps and connections of 2" and 4" plastic pipes that were interlaced all over the island and caused regular water service disruption from illegal irrigation of farm fields that were not being monitored by the utility.

The other two islands, on the other hand, had fresh potable water and septic systems for wastewater treatment. The power system on one island was a contract operator and generally in newer condition. The other island had an outdated set of 5Kw and 6Kw generating units that needed regular maintenance and replacement.

The primary focus of the utility was on the main island, and my work involved performing a comprehensive fiscal and operational assessment of all divisions in all three departments to determine what needed to be done to bring each department up to an acceptable standard. There was no capital program of any kind, and most repair work was reactive as opposed to planned maintenance and rehabilitation. I found most of the engineering staff performed all the design and contract preparation for water and wastewater distribution facilities and pumping stations to be effective and committed to the utility's success. However, the Chief Engineer was a bit arrogant and self-centered to the point that he was a liability more than an asset. After a series of poor judgments on his part and my on-site evaluations of the findings, he resigned to other opportunities, and the deputy engineer was promoted to acting chief and served very well with the full support of his staff.

Over the course of my time there, I was able to prepare an initial capital program with a two-year projection. I turned that into a six-year capital program with a Federal commitment to raise annual funding from $7 million to $20 million per year for water and wastewater distribution lines. I also garnered support from the Territory's congressional representative a separate Congressional budget line item of $10 million to bring the two wastewater plants up to their original design parameters. In my last year on the island, I garnered a funding commitment for a desalination facility once the water loss estimate got below 25 percent. The utility was down to a water loss of 40 from 65 percent, and the water system had been available 24/7 since year two of my involvement.

Over the course of my time on the island, I was the primary writer, policy analyst, strategic planner, and negotiator with financial institutions and the legislature, with the full support and backing of the Executive Director. The senior leadership team was coming along and learning the value of developing customer service relationships, building legislative support using solid data deliverables, and using trust in reporting to improve public sentiment for the utility.

The real test of the utility and our leadership team was during the three typhoons that came through the island chain, with one having the highest windspeed ever recorded at 265 mph over an 8-hour period. The utility had an emergency response team divided into public reporting, operational response, supply and logistics, and co-ordination with FEMA, EPA, DOI, and DOE, along with the central government's Emergency Management Team. It was amazing how the utility was able to get the island up and running within six months of my first experience down to three days, with the improvements to our facilities completed prior to the third event. We were able to take advantage of FEMA funding and a strong connection with supply elements from the mainland to upgrade wooden utility poles to cement poles to improve durability and long-term sustainability. FEMA agreed to fly in cherry picker trucks on an Antonov to help rebuild the secondary power distribution system, and to replace old metal water tanks with new concrete water tanks. We also up-sized the primary water supply pipelines serving neighborhoods such that water availability rose from 8 hours per day to 24 hours on a consistent basis.

With regard to the Board of Directors, it was well known that corruption was a real concern in governmental offices across the island and the legislature. Payments to the Governor and state legislators for the allowance of a Chinese corporation to build a French-styled casino and hotel were well-known and under investigation. Our Board had to be replaced in full when the Governor learned of my letter, which I was asked to present to a legislative committee on infrastructure needs, that detailed an effort by them to earn kick-backs from a financial firm wanting to finance a new power plant, which was sorely needed. This action set back the decision to commit by several years.

Our legislative agenda included working closely with the Governor's Office to assist military efforts of the Navy, Air Force, and Marine Special Forces, who were committed to improving existing military facilities on one of the islands as a forward staging base and training site for jungle fighting. Negotiating for financial support to provide services to these operations was imperative and an opportunity to build in improvements long needed by funds availability which were lacking till this new effort came along.

One of the key areas of need to improve staff capacity, intellectual capacity, leadership quality, and team spirit was adding training opportunities that allowed employees to know their full value and importance to the success of the organization. Salary improvements were authorized by the Board to build brand loyalty and family planning improvements to support growing costs of living impacts.

Lessons Learned from US Territory Island Experience:

I never realized how much could be achieved at a location so distant from mainland service options as I found on this island. Without a doubt, using local staff and building their capabilities was the only way to get control of the utility's problems. The Executive Director was wise enough to learn from me and accept my input on a variety of subjects. He gave me free rein to manage communication directly with a U.S. Congressman, the Governor, the Legislative committees, the Federal Court judge, and others because he trusted my judgment and regularly saw the favorable outcome of my activities. I feel that I made a major difference to the island's general quality of life and then to the long-term sustainability of the utility.

THE MORAL OF THE STORY

Over the course of my professional life, I have found myself dumbfounded by the lack of drive by a good many senior managers and leaders who fail to pressure staff to be movers and shakers of regular change. There is a general reluctance to introduce progressive initiatives that improve the operational imperatives of the organization to the benefit of themselves and the communities they serve because it may involve new funding needs. The analysis demonstrates the ultimate cost savings by acting and pressuring a new initiative is not being done effectively, which makes the argument for pursuing change. I always questioned how these leaders could be appointed to roles clearly out of their realm of risk-taking, moral obligation, and/or ethical guidelines. Yet, this is a norm that is repeated because there is a corporate desire by some Councils hiring City Managers, Managers hiring Division Heads, and so on to not hire someone who may rock the boat but can be loyal to a fault regardless of questionable foundational guidelines that should have been pushing for regular steps toward improvement.

It is my belief that leaders who may be reluctant to take a position of power and know they would be open to taking opposing positions are by their own nature capable of bringing the strength of personality to the role if asked, which may serve as a shield of personal protection from influence by corrupt or weak cracks in character by leadership. The reluctant leader who doesn't demand a position of power but, if offered, provides a character role model that earns a reputation of respect through fairness, empathy, understanding of staff concerns, listening to key advisors, listening to staff complaining about their work conditions; and willing to take risks; can achieve more success using the strength and value of team energy. This approach can allow the opportunity for success through their own moral and ethical sensitivities that many poorly functioning leaders find weak from an authoritarian perspective which misses the value of cooperation over domination. There are numerous examples of dominant personalities that lead poorly because they put their own success before the success of the larger whole, which is to the detriment of many organizations. There are also examples of reluctant leadership personalities that have defined the success of their administrations as the encouragement and pursuit of exception through their open willingness to share and embrace organizational change. This ultimately can breed success using the support of their team unity, who collectively enjoy the limelight which spotlights talented and creative risk takers with a shared vision of the future.

I have found leadership not hard to do. What you have is the confidence of character, the openness of curiosity, the knowledge that listening is more important than speaking, the importance of using what you hear to draw from your progressive experience, the decisions to consolidate what you have learned and implement the best possible solution(s) for the benefit of the organization. Being a confident communicator who knows how to define the problems you have found and airing the conditions that contribute to those weaknesses will open the door to a clarity of purpose and acceptance of change that may come with a price. There is also understanding the value of preparing the ground to allow plans to unfold your way by having a solid relationship with key members of the community, Board, other area organizations, and so on such that they don't fear or object when an impact of change occurs because they were prepared for it. From there, defining the road to a corrective action with a reasonable approach to budget impact and a return on investment generally has the potential to win over reluctant decision-makers who see value in themselves and their own future successes. At the end of the day, the team's credibility and shared values, under a respected and valued leader will be the new standard for building a successful organizational model.

It has been my philosophy throughout my professional career that anyone given a chance to lead should accept that they have a duty to leave the command structure, the facilities, and the organization they control better than when they arrived. That is your legacy.

A Final Perspective

Over the course of this historical walk through my professional experience, the message has been consistent. Lead by example; risk is acceptable up to a point; prepare well in advance for your team to be part of your plans to roll out your next new thing; don't take ownership of the new thing when it needs to be shared; be humble to the point that others will sing your praises; never miss taking advantage of opportunities when they present themselves which means being self-aware of the pulse of your organization; and always listen more than you speak.

The purpose of airing my record of accomplishments is to demonstrate that despite a series of challenging appointments, you can manage through the noise and controls that help handle individual problems. Where special interests were expected to pursue and push their own interests, policy amendments that open discussion to the light of public review can be your friend. When you see private interests taking advantage of the naive public agency capacity of many City Managers, executives, and senior managers, it may be due to their lack of experience and judgment to implement a strong monitoring system that assesses ongoing contractual obligations, which can have serious financial implications to the detriment of the public purse and the services being delivered. These are the examples included in my history and the approach taken to address and manage this problem.

Solutions are generally obvious but the path to attain that outcome is a road less traveled and can be hazardous to your professional career. But avoiding the problem is more of an issue than facing the music of that centrally ethical question, "what is the right thing to do?" At this point, the obvious answer is to move forward by pulling your resources through a team-based solution.

The example of what is the right path to fixing a problem is to look at all who are being affected by the problem.

- A budget officer finds himself with an employee who is both lazy but smart and a family member of one of the Council members. This person has an assigned office with a door and regularly sleeps at his desk despite repetitive disciplinary actions. The other finance staff are obviously annoyed with his antics, and it is impacting staff morale. The budget officer knows he'll be crucified if he fires him because he can do the work, but it's drudgery to get work product delivered by him on a timely basis. So, what to do?

- First, over a weekend, you have operations staff come in and take down the non-load-bearing walls of the employees' office. Leave everything else the same.
- The employee comes in on Monday and finds his desk now out in the open with the rest of the finance staff. The immediate impact is telling. He works diligently on his assignments. He gradually starts to talk with others which he hadn't ever done. Over a week's time, he gradually becomes more engaged with his peers and participates in office conversations.
- The cost, minimal. Embarrassment, minor. Staff morale, through the roof, improved. Headache resolved.

Not all problems are this straightforward, but the strategy is the same for most of them. In many ways, small successes are more valuable than major changes because they demonstrate that change can happen, and many of the small successes are the most annoying. Once resolved, the big stuff just doesn't seem so out of reach.

www.ingramcontent.com/pod-product-compliance
Lightning Source LLC
Chambersburg PA
CBHW051152120626
46547CB00012B/1060